FIND CLEAR, HELPFUL INFORMATION AND EXPERT ADVICE ON:

- Who gets schizophrenia
- Which treatment to choose, and where— in- or out-patient care
- How medication works—Thorazine, Prolixin, Mellaril, others
- How families can help while a patient is hospitalized and after discharge
- Where relatives can find support
- How to cope with school- or work-related problems
- What the future holds

"Living and Working with Schizophrenia will be an invaluable aid to the patients, the medical community, police, lawyers— in fact anyone whose work brings them in contact with schizophrenics."

—*Action* (publication of Canadian Mental Health Association)

In 1976, the authors of *Living and Working with Schizophrenia* initiated an exciting and innovative program at the Clarke Institute of Psychiatry in Toronto, Canada. Recognizing that relatives and friends play a major role in the management of the illness, they tried to develop positive and dynamic ways in which those in daily contact could contribute to the care of patients. In 1981, the American Psychiatric Association recognized their success with a "Certificate of Significant Achievement." This book is an outgrowth of the authors' experiences with the Aiding Families of Schizophrenics program.

LIVING AND WORKING WITH SCHIZOPHRENIA

M. V. Seeman, M.D.
S. K. Littmann, M.D.
E. Plummer, R.N.
J. F. Thornton, M.B.
J. J. Jeffries, M.B.

A PLUME BOOK

NEW AMERICAN LIBRARY

NAL BOOKS ARE AVAILABLE AT QUANTITY DISCOUNTS
WHEN USED TO PROMOTE PRODUCTS OR SERVICES.
FOR INFORMATION PLEASE WRITE TO PREMIUM MARKETING DIVISION.
NEW AMERICAN LIBRARY, 1633 BROADWAY, NEW YORK, NEW YORK 10019.

Copyright © 1982 by University of Toronto Press

All rights reserved. For information address University of Toronto Press,
63A George Street, Toronto, M5S 1A6.

Published by arrangement with University of Toronto Press.

 PLUME TRADEMARK REG. U.S. PAT. OFF. AND FOREIGN COUNTRIES
REGISTERED TRADEMARK—MARCA REGISTRADA
HECHO EN FAIRFIELD, PA., U.S.A.

SIGNET, SIGNET CLASSIC, MENTOR, PLUME, MERIDIAN
and NAL BOOKS are published by New American Library,
1633 Broadway, New York, New York 10019

Library of Congress Cataloging in Publication Data
Main entry under title:

Living and working with schizophrenia.

   Bibliography: p.
   Includes index.
   1. Schizophrenia.   2. Schizophrenics—Home care.
3. Self-help groups—Directories.   I. Seeman, M. V.
(Mary Violette), 1935–
[RC514.L567   1983]   616.89′82   83-22148
ISBN 0-452-25541-4 (pbk.)

First Plume Printing, April, 1984

   2   3   4   5   6   7   8   9

PRINTED IN THE UNITED STATES OF AMERICA

Contents

FOREWORD by Margaret Gibson / vii

PREFACE / xi

ACKNOWLEDGMENTS / xiv

PART ONE: BASIC INFORMATION

1   What is schizophrenia? / 3

2   Inpatient treatment / 14

3   Outpatient treatment / 27

4   Medications / 42

5   How relatives can help / 51

6   Support for relatives / 72

7   Work and school / 81

8 The future / 86

PART TWO: PERSONAL ACCOUNTS

9 A mother's account / 93

10 A father's account / 97

11 I am a schizophrenic / 100

12 A schizophrenic's story / 108

13 A mother's point of view / 115

14 The doctor's dilemma / 119

APPENDIX I: Agencies and services / 126

APPENDIX II: Family support groups by state / 130

SUGGESTED READING / 144

INDEX / 145

Foreword

I am schizophrenic, and I have been asked to write a foreword to this book because my first book, *The Butterfly Ward*, a collection of short stories, dealt with schizophrenia.

I believe that I have been a schizophrenic since I was a child. Schizophrenics have lucid states, but when they are not lucid, life is sheer hell: raging all day and spending the night on a bed in a semi-catatonic state, hearing voices and seeing things that no one else can hear or see, the sharp edge of a razor ripping open flesh like a ripe grape, the smell of burning flesh. And all this is you but not you – at that moment illusion is all that exists; you have opened the door into another reality to which you alone hold the keys. There are days, months, years when the world spins off its axis and no one can enter. We think we recognize someone we have known for years, we see their face in a dozen people only to realize (sometimes too late) that it is not them at all.

I began to dream in another language at approximately the age of nine (although not all schizophrenics do this), and this language was not of Earth. When this language entered the world's arena and was found to be unacceptable, I ceased speaking for seven years. There are many beings that have crowded my other-worldly state. A painting of one hangs in my living room to remind me that if there is a nemesis then the world or half-world that I have chosen to live in is indeed it.

There are certain chairs one must not sit on, knocks on doors when there is no one there, eyes mysteriously blackened in the dark of day.

I have seen Satan, an angel disguised as a taxi driver, and run through the snow in stocking feet with my three-year-old son because it was not 1976 any longer. An hourglass was overturned (it was some time during the Second World War) and planes were strafing, ready to kill. The rest of my family, my parents, sisters, and brother, were crumpled and dried like old autumn leaves. Only my son and I were left alive searching for the underground where we would be safe with others who were not the enemy. There is a sensation of sitting in a chair talking to someone and feeling that you are separate and drifting, sitting in the chair beside yourself. Limbs become detached and floating and certain colors take on special meanings as do certain objects. I realize that all these are very personal experiences and that each schizophrenic has his own private key to other worlds.

My father once said sadly, wearily, 'She has been in so many institutions that we have lost count.' There are always those, the ones that we leave behind, family. Families that wait with dying hope and patience for months, years, families who give up waiting altogether. The son or daughter, mother or father, ceases to exist except perhaps as a piece of furniture stored away in some warehouse. One thing I would like to say to families: while a schizophrenic is present, do not talk about him as if he does not exist. We are there, we are always there, we have ears just like everyone else.

There are good institutions and bad institutions, and the same can be said of psychiatrists. Psychiatry, despite Freud who made great inroads into the cerebral ridges, and despite Jung and Adler and the new man Laing, has a lot to learn. Psychiatry is Columbus in search of a key to the mind. Sometimes the key is found and a Pandora's box is opened, but then there is the further problem of dealing with the gargoyles that emerge. I was fortunate enough to have an excellent and caring psychiatrist for many years, despite the advice of one analyst who said to my family, 'Forget about her, she is hopelessly insane.' Today I am a 30-year-old single parent who owns her own house and takes care of her son, aged 6. My family did not forget that I was alive and fighting and always there. Chemotherapy has been of great help to schizophrenics. I know that without my medication (and I was taken off it once by a behaviorist psychiatrist), I can neither eat nor sleep nor function in any way at all. Without drugs I am not of this world.

With the help of a good and caring psychiatrist I have managed to make a life for myself and my six-year-old son. I have accepted my illness and used it in books, but I also do that with many experiences. I realize not every schizophrenic can write, but he can remain alive and fighting, for there are good psychiatrists and effective medications. He must take it on the jaw and pick himself up again. I know that we are a bunch of punch-drunk fighters.

I am not 'cured,' but my condition is greatly improved. I live and function on the outside. This is not to say that living on the outside of an institution is 'fun' or 'easy.' It is not. If you are a schizophrenic, you will find that the loneliness can be appalling, like living in solitary confinement. You may work with others and find that they do not talk to you, perhaps because your speech is disjointed or you are actually shy. You may live in a neighborhood for years without acquiring a single friend. It may seem that you live and move among people as one who is invisible. It will not be easy to go back to your family, for they may regard you as a stranger, as in fact you are to them. It will take them a long time to regard you as something less than an enigma. They may always regard you as an enigma. But it is all worth it. You can find pleasure in things that other people take for granted. I still take pleasure in shopping for groceries, in sitting in restaurants, in going to movies. And when you find a friend, and you will, cherish that friend, for he is better than gold. And you are as alive and valuable as anyone else in this world. It is nice to know that what you are feeling you are *really* feeling.

There is also something good and shining about this disease. It gives us a rare insight into the world that few people have. There are people who know we are alive and care. Try to let the world know that we matter. We matter a hell of a lot.

MARGARET GIBSON

Preface

Schizophrenia is a serious mental illness. The odds that a person will develop this illness at some time in his life are one in a hundred. It strikes most frequently in late adolescence or early adulthood, a time of great expectations in our lives, and it can shatter those expectations by running a prolonged and rocky course. Not only victims but also families and friends are affected by schizophrenia, each in different ways. Their sufferings are immeasurable, as are the social and financial costs to communities at large.

The illness was first described a long time ago and we know that it occurs throughout the world. We do not yet, however, understand precisely the cause or causes of schizophrenia, although research is progressing rapidly. In the early years of studying schizophrenia, researchers explored all possibilities – physical factors, genetic inheritance, biochemical aberrations, social factors, and psychological explanations. Investigation today still ranges just as widely. And since the schizophrenic's distress is often accompanied by disruption in the lives of the members of his family, some researchers concluded that the family disruption came first. They maintained that schizophrenic symptoms arose as an attempt to ward off the disrupt-ing influence of family members. This led to the false conclusion that the family played a causative role in the illness – a heavy burden for the family to bear.

Even without this, the condition imposes an extraordinary burden on the person afflicted and on the family he belongs to. Since the family, by and large, continues to assume the largest management and support role in the individual's prolonged struggle against schizophrenia, it is time for the health and social service professions to stop alienating families by drawing false conclusions about the cause of schizophrenia and, instead, to increase and bolster family resources. At long last, professional efforts are now being made to organize support systems for families of schizophrenics.

The authors, who have all been actively involved in the care and study of schizophrenic patients both in hospitals and in private offices, began to address this problem through the establishment of relatives' groups. Recalling similar work done with families of tuberculosis patients earlier this century, we assumed that groups could play an educational, a supportive, and a motivational role for the relatives and friends of schizophrenics. It became clear to us in the groups that many relatives (and patients) had little accurate information about schizophrenia: about its origin, manifestation, course, treatment, outcome, and risks.

Understandably, in the past health professionals, faced with their own uncertain knowledge about all these aspects of schizophrenia, were reluctant to speak freely and openly to patients and relatives about the illness. They felt, for the most part, that 'the less you mention, the less it hurts.'

This approach, we feel, needs to be modified, and our efforts at organizing groups of relatives, holding public meetings, and writing this book – all with the express aim of talking more openly about schizophrenia – are attempts to restructure attitudes towards this illness.

This book is composed of many questions and answers – all of which arose in our clinical work with patients and relatives. Also included, in part two, are autobiographical accounts of problems and solutions.

We have chosen, quite arbitrarily, to refer to the patient as 'he,' although, it must be made clear, women are as prone to the illness as men.

We hope that this book will be of most help to those who already have first-hand knowledge of what it is like to live with schizophrenia but who feel a need to know more. It is not a textbook, but a practical reference book for those whom professionals sometimes refer to as 'lay people.' In real life, it is those very lay people who can and do, on a daily basis, contribute to smoothing the path towards a happier life for the schizophrenic patient. Professionals, in contrast, monitor and advise from the more remote locations of their hospitals, clinics, and private offices.

We express our deep appreciation to the patients and relatives who contributed to this book. We are particularly grateful to those who came to group meetings, asked questions, and demanded answers.

Acknowledgments

Many, many individuals have contributed to this book. Special thanks go to Ms Margaret James, Ms Judi Levene, the Clarke Institute Parents and Friends of Schizophrenia, Mrs Claire McLaughlin, and Ontario Friends of Schizophrenics.

PART ONE
Basic information

ONE

What is schizophrenia?

How was schizophrenia discovered?

The name *schizophrenia* was introduced in 1911 by a Swiss psychiatrist, Eugen Bleuler. In 1896 a German psychiatrist, Emil Kraepelin, had christened the illness *dementia praecox* (early madness), thinking it led to a deterioration of the personality at a fairly early age. Bleuler disagreed. He observed that a loss of mental functions did not invariably develop. The new name, *schizophrenia*, comes from the Greek *skhizo*, to split, and *phren*, mind. Bleuler wanted to emphasize a basic disconnectedness or split in the personality. This split could take the form of a faulty association of ideas, an inappropriate expression of emotion, and/or a detachment from reality. It is now considered that schizophrenia is a variety of illnesses in each of which there may be somewhat different symptoms and for which the causes may also be different.

Who can become schizophrenic?

Everyone, in any part of the world, has a 1 per cent chance of developing schizophrenia sometime in his life. The manifestations of the illness, however, are to some extent influenced by the culture a person lives in. Thus, the false belief (delusion) that one is Jesus is much more likely to be held by someone in a Christian culture; the impression of being controlled by external electrical impulses occurs more readily in people who live in countries where there is electricity. The illness occurs in both sexes and makes its first appearance most commonly when an individual is in his early twenties. There are rarer forms that appear in early childhood or in much later life. The illness occurs in all walks of life, but once affected, people tend to drift downwards socially and often end up living in the poorer sections of their communities. In part, this is a result of moving away from home to be independent, and suffering the consequences of unemployment, recurrent hospitalization, and loss of vocational skills. Poverty and hardship are associated with the illness but do not seem to cause it.

What is an illness?

An illness shows itself through symptoms and signs. Symptoms are unpleasant, painful, or unusual experiences; occasionally, though rarely, they are pleasurable and produce an unrealistic sense of well-being. Signs, in contrast, are changes in behavior or demeanor that can be noticed by others. Both symptoms and signs may be physical or psychological or both. They may occur suddenly and may be severe; they are then called *acute*. Or they may develop insidiously, sometimes over a number of years. When they remain for a long period of time they are called *chronic*. A chronic condition happens most often after the individual has experienced several acute episodes.

Another way of looking at the symptoms and signs of schizophrenia is to label them *positive* or *negative*. For example, the hearing of voices when there is no one speaking in the vicinity (hallucination of hearing) or severe agitation are positive changes: though unwelcome, they are *additions* to the person's usual behavior. Negative changes are losses, such as the lessened drive to get things done or the diminished ability to derive pleasure from social activities. Studies have shown that the positive symptoms are more likely than the others to ease with medical treatment.

What are the main features of a schizophrenic illness?

To diagnose schizophrenia is not always an easy task because the features show up gradually and are not dramatic. The diagnosis can be made with confidence only when the patient is fully alert. Symptoms may include:

Delusions: A person may have an absolutely certain conviction (*delusion*), without accompanying change of mood, a) that his thoughts are being influenced, controled, inserted into his head, and/or broadcast; b) that events around him have particular significance for him; c) that he is being persecuted or treated unfairly, discriminated against, or subject to special treatment not accorded to his peers; d) that he has special powers or importance; and/or e) that his body is changed or distant or is being moved or influenced by an outside agency.

Auditory hallucinations: A person may imagine a) that his thoughts are being spoken aloud; b) that a voice is talking about him, commenting on his behavior, and/or c) that a voice or voices are talking to him.

Disturbances of feeling: A person may exhibit a) incongruous or inappropriate feeling, eg laughing when talking about sad events; b) flatness of affect, meaning that his range of emotion is limited; and/or c) loss of ability to make or maintain personal relationships.

Physical symptoms: These can include a) a slowness of movements, withdrawal, and reclusiveness; b) severe over-excitement or ecstasy; c) adoption of strange postures and manneristic behavior. (The last two have, for unknown reasons, become increasingly rare over the last twenty-five years.)

A distinct break in the patient's life: This can take the form of a definite behavioral or personality change.

A diagnosis of schizophrenia is not readily considered when there is marked sadness and depression or when there is evidence of recent drug use, especially of LSD or amphetamines. It must, of course, be realized that such drugs are sometimes used by the schizophrenic to alleviate subjective distress. They may, at times, help to bring on the illness where a predisposition to schizophrenia already exists.

The diagnosis is often easier when the onset of changes in behavior is acute. Unfortunately, there is also some evidence that the person who becomes ill more slowly and insidiously is also the one who responds less well to the various methods of treatment used today.

Accurate diagnosis requires professional training and experience.

What are the causes of schizophrenia?

Much has been written about the probable causes of schizophrenia. Many theories have had to be discarded because they were arrived at too quickly, without proper scientific inquiry.

For example, in Victorian times, some seriously blamed masturbation for the development of all kinds of insanity including schizophrenia. Other theories blamed improper nutrition and advocated large doses of vitamins. Other researchers thought they found a cause in faulty communications within families; later it became clear that problems in communication (eg the 'double bind' – a message from one person to another containing contradictory expectations) could be found in practically all families. The discovery of a so-called *pink spot* on the chromatographs obtained from the urine of schizophrenic patients created great hopes of a chemical breakthrough. It later became clear that the pink spot was related to the hospital diet of the patients tested.

Researchers follow many alleys: some lead forward, most do not. However, a few theories are generally accepted: for example, a predisposition or vulnerability to schizophrenia may be passed from one generation to another (see page 12). Since the symptoms usually first appear in the second or even third decade and not at birth, an age-specific hormonal or developmental trigger is required for schizophrenia to occur.

Can stress cause schizophrenia?

There is little doubt that stress frequently contributes to the initial appearance or subsequent recurrence of illness. For example, careful studies have shown that a schizophrenic relapse frequently occurs in someone who is threatened with the loss of his job. Such a relapse is also more likely when the person lives in a highly charged emotional environment where he is frequently exposed to critical evaluation from those around him. Such stress produces stomach ulcers in one person, skin rashes in another, alcoholism in a third, and schizophrenia in yet others. The current theory about the cause of schizophrenia is that stress produces biochemical changes in the body that the brain cells cannot deal with adequately. Current research focuses on a transmitter substance in the brain known as dopamine. Some researchers suspect that certain brain cells in the schizophrenic may be extra-sensitive to dopamine; others suspect that some of the necessary mechanisms to neutralize dopamine are lacking. As of today, it seems that schizophrenia has a definite physical basis, but that its onset may be triggered by stress.

The outlook is not nearly as grim as some authors have suggested. For the patient and his family, it is important to learn about the illness, for they can then cope more effectively. All those involved – patient, family, friends, therapists – should be clear about what the illness is and what it is not and about what it implies about the past, the present, and the future. When patients, families, friends, and therapists act together the outlook is more favorable.

To tell or not to tell?

Many doctors, themselves uncertain, do not tell patients and family members that the diagnosis may be schizophrenia. The schizophrenic may, for example, exhibit signs that are indistinguishable from those related to certain drug-induced states experienced with LSD or amphetamine psychosis. Or the schizophrenic-like behavior may be an isolated reaction which, once over, never recurs. Until a firm diagnosis is reached many doctors prefer not to talk openly about schizophrenia in order to save patients and families needless worry and concern. Yet experience has shown us that patients and families worry when they do not know. They are entitled to know at least the diagnostic possibilities, to be fully and expertly informed of the best preventive and treatment measures available, and to gain a hopeful and realistic view of the future, both immediate and long-term.

9 What is schizophrenia?

Even when the diagnosis is certain, many clinicians are hesitant to share this information with the patient and his family. They maintain that this particular diagnosis is still so ill understood that informing the family of a schizophrenic may be harmful. It may provoke completely wrong conclusions. In the same way, some doctors are reluctant to use the word *cancer* for the more treatable types of cancer because the word itself has such ominous connotations that the individuals involved become needlessly frightened. It is of course essential, when giving the diagnosis, to explain the illness and to stress the range of severity with which schizophrenia may strike. While it may make a person very ill indeed, in many instances it may be mild. It must also be explained that present-day treatments, while not cures, alleviate most of the symptoms and allow a qualitatively satisfying life. A full explanation is usually better than attempts at concealment.

Some diseases have developed a 'shameful' connotation, as if they were the results of poor hygiene or of sinful acts, something to be hidden from public view. Leprosy used to have this connotation before the world realized, through the work of Albert Schweitzer in Africa and Mother Teresa in India, that lepers are human beings and that the disease is relatively non-contagious, eminently curable, and definitely not the result of sin. Some infestations and 'social diseases' share this connotation of shame, as do certain mental disorders. While doctors themselves should not find any disease shameful, they are often sensitive to the public's view and make up names for some diseases to protect the patient from needless humiliation. It is for this reason that individuals ill with schizophrenia may be told that they have suffered a 'nervous breakdown,' are 'under stress,' are 'suffering from exhaustion,' are 'going through an identity crisis,' or have a 'functional psychosis' or a 'reactive psychosis.' There are many other words and phrases that are used to protect the patient from a diagnostic label that is thought to be shameful.

Our work has taught us that there is nothing shameful about schizophrenia. We would like the patient and his family to get to know about it.

Some individuals refuse to use the diagnosis of schizophrenia because in some parts of the world political dissidents have been sent to mental hospitals, their 'illness' labelled officially as schizophrenia. In most parts of the world, however, the medical profession realizes that the illness, even though it affects the mind and the whole personality, is in many respects a diagnosis like pneumonia, rheumatic fever, or some other medical disorder. An ethical doctor would not use it to wield power or to repress unwelcome opinions. While it has in some quarters developed connotations of hopelessness, intractability, or shame, such a response is, for the most part, quite unjustified by modern experience.

When we refer in this book to schizophrenia or to schizophrenic we speak in the same way as we might when talking about diabetes and diabetic. In the same way that the statement 'He is diabetic' describes only that aspect of the person that has to do with a specific disease and his reactions to it, so 'He is schizophrenic' refers only to an individual's specific illness and his reactions to it. It says nothing about his personality, his intelligence, his morals, his interests, or any of the countless other qualities that make this person unique. It refers to an illness which, however unfortunate, can frequently be controlled and which may, in the future, be overcome. Before starting the book proper, we would like to deal with the two most frequently asked questions: Is a normal sex life possible for the schizophrenic? and Should schizophrenics have children?

Is a normal sex life possible?

Sexual performance is not disturbed in schizophrenia, nor are sexual feelings and urges. What may frequently be disturbed is the ability to conduct a courtship. The illness often strikes in adolescence or early adulthood before dating and social skills are fully developed. After the acute illness, it is sometimes difficult to make up for the critical time lost. A person's confidence may be temporarily shattered, and he may feel unlovable.

This lack of confidence is hard to overcome, which is perhaps the reason why the majority of people with schizophrenia never marry. This is truer for men than for women, since the man, traditionally, needs to take charge in dating and courting. Especially for those who do not marry, shyness and lack of opportunity make sexual relationships difficult though courtship training and sex education can help overcome this difficulty.

Some people find that the excitement and emotional stimulation of interpersonal sexuality trigger symptoms of schizophrenia. They may learn to avoid interpersonal sex and to satisfy their sexual urges through fantasy and masturbation. The anxiety of being intimate with another person can be alleviated by behavioral methods, by discussion, and sometimes by medication. Therapy with one's partner and role-playing exercises have also been found helpful. Sexual fantasies can – as can anything – become part of delusional (unreal) thinking in schizophrenia. It may then seem as if sexual urges are so much a part of the schizophrenia that they cannot be separated out. Psychotherapy can help to preserve healthy sexual urges and to free them from being tangled up in unreal thinking.

The drugs that are used in schizophrenia have some effect on the hormones. If this affects sexual functioning it should be discussed with the doctor. A different medication can then be tried.

Women on anti-psychotic medicines occasionally do not menstruate. As long as the woman knows that this is a side-effect it should not cause concern. It does not mean that she cannot conceive. The various methods of making sure that an unwanted pregnancy does not occur should be discussed openly with the doctor.

Schizophrenia and childbearing

There is about one risk in a hundred that any child, born any time, anywhere, will develop schizophrenia as an adult, and there is at present no method of detecting the at-risk child. We do know, however, that this risk rises to one in ten if one of the parents has had a schizophrenic illness. If both mother and father have been ill with schizophrenia, the risk becomes four in ten. In other words, there is a 40 per cent chance that a child born to parents both of whom have had a schizophrenic illness will also develop schizophrenia. Although it is not known exactly how schizophrenia is passed from generation to generation, it is clear that the inheritance of a predisposition to the disease plays an important role. We know that the natural children of schizophrenic parents, even if adopted early in life, are more likely than the general population to develop schizophrenia. In other words, it is not *living* with the schizophrenic parent that favors the development of the disease. It is the biological inheritance. Children adopted into families where an adoptive parent becomes schizophrenic are no more likely than the general population to develop schizophrenia as adults.

In identical twins, if one twin has schizophrenia, so does the other about 40 per cent of the time. This is so whether the twins are brought up together or apart. If the twins are fraternal (non-identical) and one has schizophrenia, the other has a 10 per cent chance of being ill with it as well. This is exactly the same for a regular (non-twin) brother or sister.

In fact, the closer the blood relationship to a person with schizophrenia, the higher the genetic risk of becoming ill with the disease. If you are a brother or sister, son or daughter of a schizophrenic, your risk is approximately 10 per cent. If you are a grandchild, an aunt or an uncle, a nephew or a niece of a schizophrenic, your risk is about 3 per cent. This refers to the risk of developing the illness sometime in your life. The period of maximum risk, at least for men, is the late teens and early twenties. For women, it tends to be somewhat later: between 25 and 35. The older you are, particularly over 35, the smaller the risk of a first attack of schizophrenia.

The genetic risk to the unborn child must be considered before individuals with schizophrenia plan for parenthood. Also to be considered is hardship for the parents-to-be. Pregnancy may be stressful. Because no medicine in the first three months of pregnancy is totally safe for the baby, regular antipsychotic medication may need to be stopped. This may provoke illness in the mother. There are other physical, psychological, and financial strains during pregnancy and at the time of childbirth. Childbirth frequently triggers a schizophrenic episode in the mother. The demands that infants make on parents are continuous and this kind of non-stop responsibility is very hard for most people with schizophrenia. Unless there are substantial family and financial supports, being a parent is an exceptionally difficult task for individuals who have suffered with schizophrenia.

TWO

Inpatient treatment

Is hospitalization always necessary?

Hospitals are not as a rule considered happy places. Most people do not like the idea of leaving their home and entering the hospital. No matter what the illness, hospitalization is an exceptional step.

Why then admit a schizophrenic to the hospital? A doctor may recommend admission to hospital because the patient has an acute and severe illness that requires intensive observation and care. Or the patient may exhibit signs and symptoms that the doctor cannot readily explain or that constitute a possible risk to safety and health. Even when the person is not acutely ill, the doctor may arrange an elective admission in order to observe and study the illness. The general advantages of hospitalization are expert observation and care for an acutely ill patient and investigation of less acute symptoms in a planned and systematic manner. In psychiatry, the hospital is also used to 'cool things,' for example, when a serious quarrel has disrupted family life. At other times, patients are admitted to hospital simply because they are homeless and in need of shelter. Criteria for hospital admission differ somewhat from community to community, and from hospital to hospital.

All these considerations may be involved in deciding whether or not a schizophrenic should be admitted to hospital. Outpatient assessment and treatment are possible, provided that the condition is not too severe, the doctor has a good appreciation of the situation, and the doctor and patient know each other well. However, a person experiencing the first attack of acute schizophrenia is apt to be very disorganized and frightened; his behavior can be quite bizarre and upsetting. Predictions of dangerousness to self or others are difficult to make. Inpatient treatment in such conditions is desirable. But to be admitted, a person must agree to enter the hospital. If he disagrees, the doctor will have to decide whether, without hospital care, there is risk of serious physical self-harm or serious physical harm to others.

Legal requirements must be met before a person can be hospitalized against his will. The necessary conditions vary from country to country, from province to province, and state to state. By and large, the criteria have become increasingly strict over the last few years. In most communities, there must be evidence of serious mental illness and the risk of physical harm before an unwilling person can be admitted. Involuntary admissions are made only on the recommendation of a physician, who will rely on his examination of the patient and on the details furnished by the family. Admission, however, is not the same as treatment. Admitted patients may still refuse treatment. In countries with advanced mental health legislation, *treatment* against a person's will requires approval of an appeal board, although in emergencies the nearest relative may be asked for permission to administer a given treatment (see page 75).

The hospital staff

Wards vary in size. There are single and multi-bed rooms, and some hospitals still have dormitories. The ward is usually built around the nursing station, which is in the charge of the head-nurse. Each ward also has a sitting room and eating facilities, as well as group and recreation rooms and shower and washroom facilities. Psychiatric wards, by and large, are not very private places.

The staff belong to various health disciplines. They include registered nurses and nursing assistants, clinical psychologists and social workers, occupational and recreational therapists. They usually work under the overall direction of a qualified psychiatrist. Team-work has become the norm, with each team responsible for a small number of patients, and with each patient assigned for his main therapy to one or more team members. In teaching hospitals, psychiatric residents will be much in evidence. They are qualified medical doctors who are undergoing specialty training in psychiatry. Students of other disciplines (medicine, social work, occupational therapy, psychology, and divinity) also spend some of their time attached to a psychiatric ward. In addition to the staff team, there is the support staff, which includes secretaries, receptionists, kitchen personnel, cleaners, and, in some instances, security personnel. Most staff offices are located on or near a ward, but this varies from hospital to hospital.

The routine of a ward is a reflection of the team orientation and of the philosophy of the hospital. One of the basic routines deals with the necessity of creating an environment which, although artificial and restrictive, is nonetheless health-promoting. In addition, there is the need for observation of patients who may at times be very ill and at risk. There is often a system of ward privileges. This system defines the degree of freedom of the individual patient on the ward. The very ill patient may be restricted to his room, with a staff member present on a round-the-clock basis. At the other extreme is the patient who may come and go as he pleases as long as he informs the staff of his plans.

When a patient enters such a ward system, it is important

for him and his family to be given information about the ward routine. When this is not done early on, unwelcome surprises are sometimes in store, for patient, family, and staff alike.

The initial examination

On admission to the ward, the patient can expect both a physical as well as a psychiatric examination by a doctor. The psychiatric examination may last an hour or more and is intended to allow the doctor or therapist to get a comprehensive view of the person's circumstances and, in particular, of recent changes. It will include questions about the onset and development of the illness, family relationships, school or work, health record, and treatments received before. Most importantly, an attempt is made by the doctor to understand how the patient's mind and feelings are working at that particular time. This is done partly by observation and simple questions and by a number of more searching questions, some of them quite personal. Psychological tests may later be administered by clinical psychologists to help the clinician in his diagnosis and in the planning of appropriate treatment.

The physical examination is a general check of all bodily systems, but specialized examinations may be recommended where appropriate and these are then performed by other consulting specialists. Blood and urine are tested routinely. Additional tests such as X-rays, electrocardiograms, electro-encephalograms (brain-wave recordings), and brain scans may be carried out. They are indicated when symptoms overlap with those of other medical conditions or when there is an unexpected response to treatment.

Relatives or friends who accompany the patient to the hospital may be interviewed. The information they give is used in trying to understand the illness and the patient's social relationships.

Some hospitals have a special admission ward; after an initial period there, the patient may be transferred to a longer-stay ward.

The diagnosis

Usually schizophrenia is fairly easy to diagnose by the time somebody is hospitalized. In fact, the diagnosis may already have been made. On occasion, there is uncertainty, and the patient may need a period of observation. There is no specific test for schizophrenia and there may be times when the doctor is not absolutely sure of the diagnosis. The patient and family need to trust their doctor's judgment, so, if they have doubts, they should ask for a second opinion. A good doctor will always be willing to have another doctor offer a second opinion.

Some doctors, however, are not at ease when it comes to sharing a diagnosis of schizophrenia with their patients, believing that the information may upset them. In our experience it is probably more upsetting to be kept in the dark for any length of time or to be left imagining that the doctor does not know what is wrong. Sometimes, the doctor is willing to share the diagnosis, but the patient is not willing to accept it. It is, after all, not easy to accept that one is 'mentally ill.' It is very important for the patient to know that schizophrenia is an illness, that it is treatable, and that his co-operation will hasten the recovery process.

The choice of treatment

Usually, the admitting doctor decides on a provisional plan of management and treatment. It may include any or all of: medication, activity programs, behavioral programs, group and individual discussions, and general observation and supervision. Within a few days of admission there is a meeting of staff members involved in the patient's care, and a comprehensive plan of treatment is drawn up. One of the staff will then meet with the patient to discuss this plan and its implications and to seek his reactions and co-operation. Not infrequently, the patient himself has good ideas about what will be of help to him and should feel free to draw attention to these ideas.

Medication

Chapter 4 describes the role of drug therapy in schizophrenia and gives detailed information about the various types of medication currently in use, as well as about dosages.

Other physical methods of treatment

Electroconvulsive therapy (ECT)

Electroconvulsive treatment (electroshock therapy) has had something of a bad press in recent years, particularly under the impact of movies such as *One Flew Over the Cuckoo's Nest*. It is, however, a safe and humane treatment that has been found to be particularly effective for people with severe depressions. It may also help some schizophrenics, especially those who respond poorly to drugs and who, as the result of their disordered thinking and feelings, are severely disorganized or suicidal. Physical complications are very rare since great care is given to a thorough physical examination of the patient prior to treatment and to good general anaesthesia, including muscle relaxation. While patients may experience memory loss during the course of the treatment, the memory usually returns to normal within about two weeks. Modern ECT machines use less current and cause only mild and transitory memory disturbances. The treatment is controversial in schizophrenia. Some experts claim that medications make ECT unnecessary. ECT requires the written consent of the patient.

Miscellaneous physical treatments
Many treatments have been used for schizophrenia. These have included hot baths and cold baths, wet packs and dry packs (a pack is a sheet wrapped around the individual to keep him immobile), insulin coma, and a vast variety of drugs and diets. All of these have now been discarded. New treatment ideas always arise and they must be investigated because they may turn out to be breakthroughs. Three current new ideas are starvation, dialysis, and penicillin. All three of these seem highly unlikely to produce any positive results but they are all being field-tested. Families should be wary of novel, untested treatments because they may delay the beginning of effective therapy. If experimental treatments are offered, families should ask for a second opinion.

Psychological treatments

Understanding and acceptance of the condition and reassurance from others are important ingredients of hospital care. Initially, unnecessary stimulation is avoided. Gradually, more responsibility and decision-making are introduced. In some instances, psychosocial and behavioral programs help the patient to reintegrate to society by systematically rewarding socially appropriate behavior.

Family treatment

Hospitalized patients with a diagnosis of schizophrenia can be considered in three ways: 1) those who respond to medication and progressively improve until they are able to resume their normal lives, 2) those who respond to medication (in that their symptoms remit) but have other problems that delay their return to normal routines, and 3) those who do not respond to medication and their symptoms only partially or temporarily disappear.

In the first situation, regular discussions about the nature and treatment of the illness, the effect on the family, and plans for discharge seem to provide the most productive approach to family treatment.

In the second situation, patients and/or families may have had problems prior to the onset of the illness. These would not normally have led them to seek psychiatric treatment or counselling. However, the illness adds so much stress that these problems become magnified and at times seem insurmountable. Family therapy, which helps to make clear how family members affect each other, can help the patient and family to resolve these difficulties and to resume a more normal life.

In the third situation, two steps are usually followed. First, a thorough medical evaluation is attempted, to determine whether any complicating factors are operating or whether changes in the medical management are indicated. Second, there is a thorough family evaluation. Sometimes the content of the patient's hallucinations and delusions can be related, often in symbolic ways, to issues and concerns of the whole family, and the patient may thus be unwilling to 'give them up.' For example, sometimes getting better involves an acceptance that one member of the family has a serious illness that requires continued medication, and this may be particularly difficult for the patient and family to accept. Sometimes the roles of 'patient' and 'caretaker' become so entrenched in families that they are difficult to change, and sometimes the symptoms of the patient upset one or more family members and thereby complicate the picture. In these situations, family therapy can 'free up' the patient and/or other family members from non-productive behavior. The patient may then be more responsive to treatment, including medication or psychotherapy. There can be a very complex relationship between physiological and psychological factors. While psychotic symptoms, such as feelings of persecution, are caused by biochemical factors, the *content* of the delusions may be related in exaggerated or symbolic ways to concerns shared by other family members, for example, that it is the police (or Communists, Martians, or Freemasons) who are doing the persecuting.

Financial affairs

As a rule, hospitalized psychiatric patients are able to maintain control of their finances, although hospital regulations usually demand that valuables or large sums of money be deposited in the hospital business office for safe-keeping. When the psychiatric disorder is of such a degree and nature that irreparable financial harm may result, the psychiatrist has the power to declare the person financially incompetent. The patient's assets, then, are managed by a private committee or by the public trustee (see page 68).

Visiting regulations

Psychiatric wards welcome visitors and have generous visiting hours. Restrictions apply at certain times so as to avoid interference with ward programs such as therapy, meals, and sleep. However, visiting hours and rules depend upon the philosophy of the ward and its patient population, with a good deal of variation from ward to ward. On some occasions, visiting may be seriously disturbing to the patient or to the visitor, and the staff may temporarily suspend visits or limit their duration.

It may happen that the visiting family or friends may hear complaints about his treatments from the patient. These complaints should be discussed with the staff. They may be a product of the patient's illness, a result of misunderstanding between patient and staff, or may be due to a failing on the part of the staff which must be remedied. Families, when in doubt, should ask for a second opinion from a psychiatrist outside the hospital. Alternatively, they may ask for a transfer to another facility.

Passes

A patient whose illness is not too severe is given the opportunity to leave the hospital to spend a weekend with family or friends, to go out to dinner or a show, or to attend significant family functions. The success of these outings reflects the extent to which recovery has progressed. Whether a patient is ready to resume the activities of everyday life can be judged by how well the visits go. After an outing, it is important for the patient to report back his observations about how well he managed. If anything significant did occur it is often helpful for the family or friends to let the staff know.

As a general rule, a pass should be seen as part of a gradual convalescence and not as an intense social engagement. Whenever necessary, guidance should be sought from the ward staff as to what is advisable. It is safer for a patient on medication not to drive, drink, or go near machinery when on a pass unless specifically given permission to do so by the treating physician.

Of course, not every outing goes smoothly and if the patient feels upset or if his behavior is disturbing to those with whom he is spending his time, it is perfectly appropriate to return to the hospital early rather than let things get out of control.

Other illnesses

All psychiatric units have arrangements available for medical and surgical consultation at short notice, and the patient is usually assured of competent medical help for any other illness that occurs while in the hospital.

Discharge planning

A short hospital stay is generally to be preferred, because people who are hospitalized for a long time have great difficulty in returning to their previous level of activity. This is true whatever the illness. Too often, passivity is induced by a hospital stay and can make being an 'invalid' attractive and resuming the full activities of life unappealing. However, some patients respond rather slowly to treatment. The psychiatric staff has very difficult decisions to make in balancing adequate control of the symptoms and speedy discharge.

The final decision about discharge is based on a number of factors. These include the degree to which the symptoms have disappeared, the patient's social functioning on his weekend passes, and the extent to which an adequate follow-up has been organized. The length of stay varies a great deal. The average for a first schizophrenic illness is from three to six weeks.

It is also very important for the staff to consider the emotional environment to which the patient will return. Recent research has shown that patients who return to homes where there is a high degree of emotional expression, particularly of a critical nature, break down and return to the hospital more readily. However this is true only when the patient is spending a lot of time at home in close contact with family members. Too much closeness may be a cause of tension and upset for all the family (and not just in schizophrenia). It is not a cause of schizophrenia, but it can lead to stress and breakdown and readmission to hospital.

There are various ways to deal with discharge from hospital. First, the patient may decide not to return to the family home and arrangements can be made for a new living situation. Whether or not the patient *does* return home he will probably fare better if he is occupied outside the house most weekdays, for example, in a day hospital, workshop, schooling, or job. Also, in those families where there is a lot of emotion and criticism, family counseling will often help to reduce the family tension and ease the situation for all the family members.

A comprehensive discharge plan should cover medication, job planning, living arrangements, and social activity; such a program distinguishes good psychiatric care from inferior care. The plan should be drawn up by the hospital therapy team, the patient, his family, and the post-hospital therapy–community team. Families can be crucial here in examining and deciding on possible options.

Day care or evening care?

Many psychiatric wards have day care programs. These are intended mainly for patients ready to be discharged from inpatient care who may still require a period of less intense involvement. Day patients usually attend on weekdays, during working hours. In some settings they simply follow the general ward timetable. In others, a specific program has been developed for day patients with perhaps a focus on their particular problems.

A different type of day care is offered in certain specialized settings where admission to an intensive five- or seven-day-a-week day (only) care program is seen as an alternative to inpatient care. There is much to be said for such programs for they maintain people in their familiar surroundings and thus avoid the stigma that results from patients no longer being visible among their peers or friends.

Evening care is another variety of partial hospitalization. It is particularly appropriate for patients who are ready to return to work or to school, but who are concerned about their power of readjustment, especially during the first week or two after discharge from the ward. For these patients, evening or night care permits a solution. The patient is away from the ward all day, either at work or at school, and returns to the ward for the evening meal. It is desirable that special treatment programs be arranged for such patients at hours convenient to them.

Conclusion

In conclusion, many schizophrenic patients will require hospitalization at one time or another. The main reasons for hospitalization are serious risk to the patient or others around him or a need for close study and observation, including investigations. Hospitalization per se does not offer a permanent cure. The main therapeutic emphasis is on rehabilitative techniques that begin in hospital and continue long after discharge.

THREE

Outpatient treatment

Treatment in hospital is only a fraction of total treatment since schizophrenia is potentially there for the rest of a person's life. About one-third of individuals who suffer a first acute attack may never have another one. But for the other two-thirds, treatment needs to be life-long. At this stage in medical knowledge, it is impossible to distinguish those who do from those who do not require long-term treatment. Because of this uncertainty it is better to err on the safe side and to recommend outpatient treatment to everyone who has suffered an attack of schizophrenia.

In a hospital or clinic, patients are apt to have dealings with members of a treatment team as well as with other patients, some of them schizophrenic. In a private practice, the patient enters into a more exclusive relationship with his psychiatrist. In the former setting he may develop a degree of institutional reliance, in the latter a form of personal dependence.

Outpatient visits

1 If an outpatient visits a clinic or hospital regularly, doctors can monitor his medications in order to prevent readmissions

and minimize drug side-effects. (Most but not all patients will be on medication after an acute episode of schizophrenic illness.)

2 The patient can engage in an active social program in order to counteract apathy and the tendency to withdrawal.

3 He can learn progressively more about schizophrenia and how to plan a rewarding life despite the illness.

4 Visits can also enable him to benefit from individual, group, and family counseling about personal problems that may affect the illness.

5 The patient can take advantage of liaison services with schools, jobs, housing authorities, training programs, financial assistance, and recreational facilities.

Who needs to come for outpatient visits?

Everyone who has been ill with schizophrenia needs treatment as an outpatient in order to prevent the return of the illness. This includes even people who consider themselves completely recovered since they, too, may be at risk for a return of the illness. Making sure that the acute symptoms do not return usually means taking medication. Some people, in time, may find that they do not require medication. It is impossible, however, to predict in advance who these people will be. There needs to be a certain amount of trial and error to see who can do without it. A return of the original symptoms will mean that medication has to be continued. Needing medication is NOT a mark of weakness. It is a fact of life for the great majority of people with schizophrenia just as insulin is a fact of life for many people with diabetes.

A lack of energy and an aversion to being among people signal a need for outpatient treatment. The longer one isolates oneself after an acute bout of schizophrenia the harder it becomes to go out and face the world. Treatment provides occupational activity in areas of individual interest. It provides opportunities to meet people, opportunities to 'come out of the shell' in a gradual, non-pressured atmosphere with a maximum of support. Different programs do this in different ways.

Everyone who has had a schizophrenic illness needs to come to terms with what this means for the future. Many will need to have their relatives involved so that they, too, can learn about the illness and plan accordingly. Many will need help in educational, vocational, and occupational tasks – special school programs, for instance, or special sheltered workshops.

How often do people need to attend?

Frequency of outpatient visits is an individual matter that depends on the patient's needs, the flexibility of the patient's and the therapist's hours, the nature and cost of the outpatient program, and the demands and the extent of the patient's other commitments. There is no ideal frequency. In general, however, visits become less frequent as time goes on. They may start as day care, when the patient is expected to attend daily for a major portion of the working day. Later, there may be weekly visits, and eventually the intervals between visits may reach one, two, or three months.

Outpatient treatments

Medication
See chapter 4.

Remotivation
The best treatment for apathy and disinterest is remotivation. This means opening windows on life by discussion, examina-

tion of self-defeating attitudes, and gently applied pressure and reward for taking risks and trying new things. The treatment team provides a variety of non-threatening opportunities to take up former interests and revamp old skills. The results of motivational work seem often to be better when the activities are carried out in a group setting, but this may not be so for everyone.

Therapies for daily activity
As a result of schizophrenia and hospitalization, many difficulties need to be overcome and new adjustments or life strategies need to be made. Many of the following kinds of therapy are used in outpatient treatment, although not necessarily all at the same time and not always in the same place:

1 counseling or psychotherapy – individual and group – for the patient;

2 education about schizophrenia, together with realistic planning for the future;

3 counseling for interpersonal difficulties, in the form of marital therapy, family therapy, parenting groups, and other group therapies;

4 vocational and educational assessment, counseling, and re-training;

5 social therapies aimed at improved use of free time through various activities such as sports, music, dancing, and art activities (all ways to become actively reinvolved in the world);

6 teaching about and encouraging the development of self-help therapies (treatments that the patient administers himself) through assertiveness training, nutrition and hygiene clinics, budget workshops, homemaking workshops;

7 maintenance of liaison between the therapist or case manager in the mental health facility and a number of important people and agencies, such as the family, the family doctor,

and the public health nurse; employment counsellor and employer; sheltered workshops, landladies, and group-home supervisors; and community activity centres and self-help groups.

The role of the medical doctor

Any program for schizophrenia must have the active participation of a doctor. Schizophrenia is not merely a problem in living, it is first of all a medical disease. That is not to say that patients must be seen by doctors and by doctors only, but rather that doctors must be part of the program. Some family physicians are skilled at this. For the most part, however, psychiatrists who have both medical and psychiatric training are required from time to time.

Choice of medication and subsequent adjustment of dosage are skilled tasks which need constant monitoring. It is not enough simply to prescribe medication and then leave it at that. There must be frequent opportunities for reconsidering the dose and type of drug. Mental health professionals and paraprofessionals who are not doctors often, through experience, gain great expertise in monitoring medication. This happens, though, only in settings where psychiatrists are easily available for consultation. A discussion of medication appears in the next chapter; problems of long-term use are discussed on page 46.

Activity therapy

Programs must be able to counteract the apathy and social withdrawal of schizophrenia. Two elements are essential: a program that can occupy much of the patient's day; and a large enough group of helpers (including other patients) so that people do not feel alone with their handicap, and so that a community can be established whose members begin to matter to each other.

Community links

An outpatient program for schizophrenia must be connected,
by as many links as possible, to the community in which the
person lives. In order to make effective use of these agencies
when necessary, the therapeutic staff must be in continuing
contact with the family; with educational facilities; with health
facilities (family doctor, hospital clinic, dentists, dietitians,
and exercise programs); with vocational rehabilitation centres
and employment agencies; with government social agencies;
with residential facilities; with community workers (public
health nurses, police officers, community occupational therapists, visiting homemakers, mental health volunteers); with
sheltered workshops and graduated work programs; and with
leisure and social clubs for ex-mental patients. The more
familiar the staff are with what is available in the community,
the smoother the transition for the recovering schizophrenic.

Whom to see for counseling

It makes sense for one person to be the primary therapist or
counselor and to act as program co-ordinator. This person
need not be a doctor. A paraprofessional is often easier and
more rewarding to talk to. Different aspects of the program
will, however, introduce the patient to other therapists who
will be able to help in varying degrees. This will depend on
their special expertise and on individual needs. The primary
therapist can belong to any of the mental health professions
or paraprofessions such as nursing, social work, psychology,
rehabilitation, occupational therapy, psychiatry or, in certain
regions, he may be the family doctor. The primary therapist
should be someone with whom the patient finds it easy to
talk and to share problems. He need not be an expert in
everything but must be understanding enough and knowl-

edgeable enough to know when to link the schizophrenic and his family with other therapists and other therapeutic programs.

A time of distress for an outpatient often occurs when the primary therapist changes. Some programs use student trainees. This means frequent turnover when students graduate. Clients may feel disappointed by the recurrent changes; no sooner do they know a therapist than that therapist is on his way and they have to start all over again. For those not too overcome by separation, there are also a few advantages to changes in therapists. New therapists are often enthusiastic and their optimism is catching. In addition, the helplessness of profound dependency is avoided by the change, and the patient is given the opportunity to learn how to form new relationships.

Are hospital-based programs best?

This is not necessarily the case. It depends on what is available in the community.

Hospitals have both advantages and disadvantages as settings for outpatient care. They are often familiar and trusted places for individuals who have attended the hospital as inpatients. A multidisciplinary team is usually available. Staff are familiar with medication problems. There is a pharmacy and there is the equipment necessary for intramuscular injections, should they be required. There is an emergency room for people with 'off-hours' problems and staff can usually be reached twenty-four hours a day. If hospitalization becomes necessary, the patient can be admitted to a place that is familiar and not intimidating.

However, attending a hospital seems to imply that one is still ill, rather than getting better. Going to hospital for treatment sounds more serious than attending a family doctor or a community program. Hospitals can be frightening places associated with bad memories for some people.

Community-based programs often have a more home-like atmosphere and, ideally, are housed in more spacious quarters than those available to outpatient departments. They are often situated in community centres that have gymnasiums, parks, and meeting rooms available for the use of participants. Some may include a sheltered work setting or a supervised residence. Some of the advantages of hospitals (availability of doctors, injection equipment, etc) can be easily incorporated into community programs. They can function independently and not be subject to the various red-tape procedures of hospital clinics.

The treatment of schizophrenics by private practitioners is an important part of overall community care. It calls for a degree of selectivity on the part of the clinician since patients who are too disturbed, or who lack adequate social supports, are more effectively looked after in a clinic. Good communications between private practitioners and the hospital services allow for more effective crisis management and after-care planning.

Does supportive treatment need to continue forever?

In some form, it probably does, although support systems vary from individual to individual.

People who have had serious health problems, and schizophrenia is a case in point, should always have easy and immediate access to health counseling. Being in treatment does not mean that the frequency of contact should continue forever as it was in the first few years following hospitalization. Staying in touch, perhaps by telephone only, may be sufficient as time goes by. The ex-patient should always have someone whom he can call in an emergency. If the primary therapist leaves, he should arrange to be linked to someone else, even though all troublesome symptoms may have disappeared long before.

How to recognize the reappearance of illness

Schizophrenic illness has characteristic early signs and recurrent patterns.

Many people report that the original schizophrenic illness came without warning, 'out of the blue.' After the first episode, however, people have been sensitized and are more able to recognize early warning signs, even though the signs may be slow in development and vague in nature.

Each individual has his own set of early warning signs. Some frequently encountered ones are diminished ability to concentrate, increased irritability, uncontrollable moods, increased self-consciousness, difficulties in thinking, social withdrawal, increasing suspicion of other people's motives, and inability to sleep.

It is very important to recognize one's own early signs of illness and to be able to connect them with a trigger. The trigger is very often over-stimulation in its various forms, but it may also be other psychological stresses (loss of support, disappointment, rejection) or physical stresses (exhaustion, fever, alcohol, drugs). Too many life changes too quickly can precipitate acute illness. Major life changes are best spaced far apart.

How to control acute illness

Control consists of removing the trigger and increasing medication.

Recognized early, the progression of illness can be stopped by temporarily increasing the dose of medication and temporarily withdrawing from what has become an over-stimulating environment. The person with schizophrenia has to learn to avoid over-stimulation. At the same time he must learn to avoid under-stimulation, which leads to apathy and lack of initiative. This balancing act is difficult but can be learned. When acute symptoms begin to develop, it is usually a sign that work pressure must be muted, personal relationships soft-pedaled, expectations lowered, and the schedule of activities slowed. These measures, when promptly initiated, can frequently prevent hospital admission. They are, of course, *temporary* measures, to be discontinued when the crisis has passed.

Are vitamins useful?

They are not useful for schizophrenia. Most doctors feel that if diet is adequate extra vitamins are unnecessary. Large-dose vitamins (megavitamins) have been claimed to be useful in treating schizophrenia, but carefully controled studies fail to bear this out. There is no question that some people do improve, however, while taking vitamins. It may be that the improvement is due to the neuroleptic drugs (see pages 42–7) they are taking at the same time; it may be that their condition is not schizophrenia; or it may be that the patient belongs to that 30 per cent who recover and stay well. Alternatively, the structure and effort involved in co-operating with a well-balanced vitamin and diet daily schedule may in itself be therapeutic.

Are special diets necessary?

Nutrition is important to well-being but this is no more true for the person with schizophrenia than for any other individual. The general apathy that often follows schizophrenia means that little interest is taken in anything, including food. If this leads to poor nutrition, fatigue and lack of energy may well increase. This is a special problem for people living alone who do not have the motivation to prepare proper meals. A well-balanced diet should be encouraged but special diets are not necessary. Some special diets may in fact be harmful if essential ingredients of a regular diet are missing. Many people would rather diet than take medicines, and special diets for schizophrenia are frequently popularized in the press. In the last few years gluten-free diets, low-sugar diets, liquid-only diets, milk-free diets, and periodic fasts have been hailed as 'cures' for schizophrenia. These fads have no merit whatsoever.

Medication for schizophrenia may lead to undesired weight gain. Starvation diets and appetite suppressants are *not* the answer. The physician should be consulted for better solutions.

How safe are 'new' therapies?

It is best not to discontinue treatment that is 'tried and true' in favour of intriguing but as yet untested alternatives. Since there is still no 'total answer' to schizophrenia, people tend to expect too much from any new discovery as it comes along. This is a form of wishful thinking. New discoveries are steps towards the goal of understanding the disease, but each one is only a partial answer to the many problems involved. Going from doctor to doctor, city to city, looking for a miracle cure is a frustrating and ineffective way of looking after oneself.

Is psychotherapy useful?

Since psychological events (on their own) do not – as far as we know – cause schizophrenia, it is unlikely that psychological treatment on its own can cure it. However, getting to know oneself better, understanding the nature of one's problems, recognizing one's feelings, exploring one's reactions, and planning ahead realistically are all important. Psychotheraphy that promotes these activities is very useful in schizophrenia. It is not intended as a cure but as an approach to self-understanding and towards understanding events in the immediate environment which may precipitate a relapse.

Psychotherapy can be carried out between two individuals, in a group, or in a family. One form of psychotherapy may be more useful at one time; another may be preferred at another time. The use of medication does not preclude psychotherapy.

What are the dangers of alcohol and street drugs?

Alcohol and street drugs can trigger episodes of schizophrenia and should not be used. Certain cold tablets, weight-reducing pills, or even nose drops can precipitate episodes of illness. Patients can learn to be alert to the effect of chemical substances (and even foods such as coffee or spices) on their individual symptoms. Some substances (alcohol, marijuana) have an immediate relaxing effect that is experienced as soothing, but they may have a later withdrawal effect that is harmful.

Are self-help groups useful?

Organizations set up by patients for mutual support have been around for many years (for example, Recovery; Grow) and have played an important role in helping ex-patients readjust to society. More recently there has been increased development of groups concerned with patients' rights which have looked at psychiatry from the vantage point of the 'consumer' and found the profession wanting. There are still controversial areas of treatment in schizophrenia as in other illnesses, and even when the best treatment is prescribed its application may not be always carried out in the most humane manner. It is crucial that those who work in psychiatry pay careful attention to the criticisms made by the consumers.

Naturally, the people most likely to join patients' rights groups are those who personally feel they have been mistreated, and there is a danger in such groups of developing a polarized attitude, condemning a particular mode of treatment generally, whereas the treatment itself may be fine but the particular use of it inappropriate. For example, Judi Chamberlin has written a book, *On Our Own*, that has many important things to say about mental patients' associations but which categorically rejects medication: 'Drugs, euphemistically called psychiatric medication, are given to patients with the avowed purpose of changing their 'sick' thoughts, and the process is called treatment.' Her book was described as 'an honest and intelligent assault on psychiatric atrocities' by the psychiatrist Thomas Szasz, who rejects the commonly held view of schizophrenia as an illness of the brain. Contrast this with the book *Psychobattery* by Theresa Spitzer. It too is a criticism of psychiatry and psychiatrists, but attacks the use of psychotherapy in situations where medication is indicated. Both these books make valuable points as long as they are not taken to mean that all medication or all psychotherapy should be discarded.

Ideally, there should exist a mutually beneficial relationship between patients' rights groups and professionals, each with an open approach, willing to listen and to learn from one another.

Confidentiality of information

Legally and ethically no information about a patient can be shared outside a treatment team without the patient's written consent. This rule applies even when the person asking for information is obviously asking for the patient's good. In other words, even if a lawyer who wants to defend a patient requires medical information to prove his client innocent, that cannot be given without the patient's written consent. If a mother or father or spouse wants information that might make it easier for them to deal with the patient at home, that, too, cannot be given without consent. Often mental health staff appear distant and secretive to relatives because they are concerned about not revealing confidential information. Relatives and staff need to understand the need to know, on the one hand, and the need to preserve confidences, on the other.

By the same token, relatives sometimes want to tell mental health staff about the patient's behavior but want this information to be kept secret. They may find some therapists unwilling to listen to this type of confidential information because mere knowledge of facts is not judged useful unless it can be discussed openly with the patient. If the relative does not want the patient to know the source of the information, then the information may be of little use. Therapists need to appreciate that many relatives need help and support to deal with this problem. The most helpful way is for the relative to come with the patient to discuss troublesome behavior with the therapist.

Access to the clinical record

Only the treating team has access to a person's clinical record.

No one else can look at the clinical record without the written consent of the patient. The only exception to this is that researchers are sometimes given permission to study all the charts of people who, for instance, were admitted to hospital on a certain day or who share a common diagnosis or who are being treated with the same medication. Research to further medical understanding is usually part of a university hospital setting and is always under the strict supervision of the hospital/or university ethical review board. Any information recorded for research purposes is coded by number; the patient's name does not appear on the research data. If patients are interested in seeing parts of their own clinical record, they should discuss this with their doctor. Different countries, states, and provinces have different regulations on this.

Dissatisfaction with outpatient treatment

Dissatisfaction usually has to do with one or other of the following: a) the patient is not getting better; b) he suffers from side-effects of medication; c) he feels a lack of interest on the part of the therapist; d) the therapist is unavailable at a critical time; e) the therapist and patient (or relative) have different philosophies of treatment.

All these problems require discussion with the therapist. Usually satisfactory solutions can be found. If, after discussion, no resolution is reached, the patient or family is justified in asking for a second opinion or arranging for referral to another therapist. This can usually be done through the family doctor.

If the patient begins treatment with a new therapist, it is important for the new therapist to have as accurate a picture as possible of the patient's prior illness. Otherwise, an inaccurate diagnosis may be made and an inappropriate treatment plan may be put into effect.

FOUR

Medications

Introduction

Individuals with schizophrenia, and their families, sometimes find the array of different medicines used in schizophrenia bewildering. They find it hard to sort out which medicines do what.

In other chapters of this book, whenever we refer to 'medication,' we mean neuroleptics, which are anti-schizophrenic agents. Whenever we mention 'staying on medication,' 'increasing or decreasing medication,' or 'stopping medication,' we are referring to neuroleptics.

Other kinds of medicines are also used at times in the course of a schizophrenic illness: pills used for neuro-muscular side-effects of neuroleptics, hypnotics, minor tranquilizers, lithium salts, anticonvulsants, antihistamines, and antidepressants, and these, too, will be briefly discussed in this chapter.

Neuroleptics

Neuroleptics are drugs (pharmacological agents) that reverse schizophrenic symptoms. They used to be called major tranquilizers, but that name is not much used now because it gave people the wrong idea about these agents. Some of them do 'tranquilize,' but not all, and the tranquilization or sedation is a side-effect, not the effect for which they are prescribed. (Tranquilization is more a property of the so-called minor tranquilizers such as 'Librium' and 'Valium.' These are *not* neuroleptics. They are not related chemically to neuroleptics. Except under special circumstances, they are not much used in schizophrenia.)

There are about twenty neuroleptics in common use and each has several names. One name is the officially approved name and the others are 'trade names' – each drug company gives its own name to a drug. In this chapter we shall use the official name and only one or two of the more popular trade names to identify each drug. Sometimes the same chemical formula put out by different companies is priced differently. Sometimes a 100-milligram tablet, say, costs quite a bit less than two 50-milligram tablets. It is wise to price the tablets in the pharmacy and to discuss price and all other questions about medication with the prescribing doctor.

The neuroleptics come in many different chemical structures and have many different names. They all, however, act in the *same* way in schizophrenia. They all reduce the transmission of the brain chemical dopamine, which carries messages from certain specific cells in the brain to other specific cells in the brain. The reduction of dopamine results in fewer hallucinations and delusions and less illogical thinking. Exactly how this is done is unknown, but it has something to do with the nature of the nerve pathways that are under the control of the dopamine molecule. All neuroleptic molecules can assume the shape of a dopamine molecule; in this way they 'fool' the receptor for dopamine on the nerve-cell surface and prevent the dopamine from getting through and firing the cell. Neuroleptics work well for schizophrenia, but are not used for most other psychiatric conditions, such as depressions, phobias, or anxieties.

Although all neuroleptics interfere with dopamine in the same way, each has other different properties. For instance, they differ in their effects on brain chemicals other than dopamine.

Chlorpromazine ('Largactil,' 'Thorazine') also affects noradrenaline transmission. Thus it is sedating.

Thioridazine ('Mellaril') affects acetylcholine transmission and has unpleasant effects such as blurring of vision, dry mouth, and, in the male, problems with erection and ejaculation. Interference with acetylcholine transmission, however, can be useful, because the brain maintains a balance between dopamine and acetylcholine. When one goes down, there is a relative preponderance of the other. So with many neuroleptics, dopamine goes down and there is a relative upsurge of acetylcholine. This can cause tremor, muscle stiffness, muscle spasm, and motor restlessness. Thioridazine has the advantage of not producing these muscle effects because it interferes with acetylcholine as much as it does with dopamine. But, especially in older people, these effects may be harmful. Thioridazine has to be used very carefully, especially since it is given in relatively high doses. This is because it does not dissolve in the fatty substance on the surface of the nerve cell, where the chemical receptors are.

Neuroleptics such as perphenazine ('Trilafon'), trifluoperazine ('Stelazine'), fluphenazine ('Moditen,' 'Prolixin'), and haloperidol ('Haldol') dissolve easily in fats and therefore the doses can be very low. Two milligrams of haloperidol have the same anti-schizophrenic potency as 100 milligrams of chlorpromazine or thioridazine. Relatives often wonder why one person has to take so many milligrams while another takes such a seemingly small amount. In fact, the person on the smaller dose may be taking a 'stronger' anti-schizophrenic drug. Patients often wonder why they seem to have so many side-effects and other patients do not, why one person seems to improve so rapidly almost as soon as a medicine is started and another takes so long to improve. That is because each person's medication type and dose have to be individually tailored.

The type and dose of a neuroleptic that a person will respond to depend on many factors such as height and weight, activity, diet, physical health, other pills being taken at the same time, speed of digestion, extent of body fat stores, and so on. It is quite hard to predict exactly which neuroleptic a given person will respond to. Frequently a doctor will choose one on the basis of the kinds of side-effects it usually produces. In other words, if a person is feeling attacked and needs to be on guard, a doctor will avoid giving a neuroleptic that will make him sleepy or else he may feel unguarded and his fears of attack may paradoxically increase. If a person feels that his body is being controlled by outside forces then a doctor will avoid prescribing a neuroleptic that might make him feel stiff and paralyzed or else his sense of being controlled will increase.

Sometimes *depot* or long-acting medicines are used. These are neuroleptics given to last for a week or several weeks at a time. They are given as one injection, deep into the muscle. Fluphenazine decanoate ('Prolixin decanoate,' 'Modecate') is one of the more commonly used depot drugs, although in some countries there are several in common use. The advantages of this treatment is that it by-passes the digestive tract (for people who are poor absorbers). It is easier to keep track of, and patients do not have to rely on their memory in order to take their pills as prescribed. It costs less. It means that the patient comes once a week (or less often) to the clinic for his injection and, while there, may also take part in other clinic activities. For all the advantages, many doctors do not like to prescribe depot neuroleptics because it means that medication-taking becomes a passive experience for the patient. It is better, all things being equal, that the patient be active in the taking of his pills, understand how they work, and be familiar with doses, side-effects, time lags before response sets in, and so forth. The more the patient is part of the treatment, the better.

Many relatives worry about the long-term effects of medicines. Neuroleptics have now been in use for thirty years, so it is unlikely that anything new, as far as dangerous long-term effects go, will be discovered now. Some long-term effects do exist. Some people, after many years of using neuroleptics, develop skin discoloration and some opaque deposits in the cornea or lens of the eye. These do not interfere with vision. Some people, after many years of use, develop tics and spasms of muscles, especially the muscles around the face. In most cases, when the neuroleptics are stopped, these tics and spasms initially get a little worse but then they disappear. In some people though, especially older people, they do not disappear even after the neuroleptics have been stopped for some time. The reason for this is not clear. Families may find these tics a nuisance although most patients do not seem aware of them and often feel they are a small price to pay for the security of staying free of psychosis. Tics and tremors that persist after medication is stopped are called *tardive dyskinesia*, which means late-appearing disjointed movements.

Many relatives ask: 'When should medication be stopped?' No one really knows the answer to this question. Some individuals, even though they continue to have schizophrenic symptoms, can stop their pills and the symptoms will not get worse. Other individuals, though, may be free of all symptoms and feel healthy, but when the pills are stopped, they once again develop a full-fledged schizophrenic attack. This is what makes the decision about when to stop neuroleptics so difficult. Many doctors advocate a gradual reduction with close observation and detailed reporting on subjective feelings. Some patients get to know themselves so well that they can tell when symptoms are about to happen and can then, on their own, take extra medication. It usually takes many years of knowing oneself though, before this can be done well. Some doctors recommend periodic drug holidays – periods of days or weeks without medication – but for many people this may be too risky. It is wise to follow the doctor's advice very faithfully on this and all other issues related to the taking of medication.

Pills for neuro-muscular side-effects (antiparkinsonians)

Since there is a balance in the brain between the neurotransmitters dopamine and acetylcholine, the use of neuroleptics to block dopamine frequently produces a relative preponderance of acetylcholine. This leads to a state that looks like Parkinson's disease: tremor, rigidity, restlessness, expressionless face, and, sometimes, muscle spasms. These side-effects are usually short-lived and are usually easily reversible by the addition of 'anticholinergic' agents, commonly called *side-effect pills* or *antiparkinson pills*. There are many of these. Perhaps the most commonly prescribed ones are benztropine ('Cogentin'), trihexyphenidyl ('Artane'), and procyclidine ('Kemadrin'). These are not given for the symptoms of schizophrenia or for the prevention of relapse but for side-effects of neuroleptics. If the patient is not taking neuroleptics, he does not need to take these pills. If he is still taking neuroleptics but, as is usual, the initial muscular side-effects have disappeared, the side-effect pills should be discontinued. Taken by themselves, they are potentially toxic or poisonous and may produce their own side-effects. When they are first discontinued, there may be a short withdrawal reaction consisting of nausea and vomiting. This goes away in two to three days. Some muscle side-effects respond better to one type of pill and some to another. If side-effect control is not satisfactory, let the doctor know.

Hypnotics

Schizophrenics, like many other people, may have difficulties sleeping at night. For a person with schizophrenia, a full night's sleep is important and some doctors may prescribe sleeping medication. Since some neuroleptics are sedative, an increased dosage of neuroleptic at night may be sufficient. In some instances, the psychiatrist may prefer to prescribe minor tranquilizers, antihistamines, chloral hydrate, or other sleeping agents. If you have any questions about why a particular hypnotic or sleeping medication was chosen, discuss it with the doctor.

Minor tranquilizers

These are used for anxiety and are sometimes referred to as *anxiolytics*. There are many of them. The benzodiazepines 'Librium' and 'Valium' are the best known. Their mechanism of action is unclear. One idea is that they reduce anxiety by stimulating a rise in the brain levels of a neurotransmitter called gamma-amino-butyric acid (GABA). While anxiety is probably a universal phenomenon, it may be especially stressful for schizophrenics, and the psychiatrist may want to reduce it. These agents are effective for the short term but usually lose their effectiveness after a few weeks and are not commonly prescribed over long periods. There may be exceptions to this rule, however. These agents are also muscle relaxants and anticonvulsants. Sometimes they are used for the muscular side-effects of neuroleptics.

Lithium salts

Lithium ('Lithane,' 'Carbolith') is used to stabilize mood. Mood is not usually the main problem in schizophrenia but may well be an additional one, so lithium may be used in conjunction with neuroleptics. Some individuals with schizophrenia do not respond to neuroleptics but do well with lithium.

Anticonvulsants

Schizophrenics do not usually experience convulsive seizures, but there are individuals who suffer from a combined form of schizophrenia and epilepsy. For them neuroleptics may be prescribed with anticonvulsants, of which there are many. The most commonly used one is phenytoin ('Dilantin'). A few people with schizophrenia do not respond to neuroleptics but do well with an anticonvulsant.

Antihistamines

These are anti-allergy pills distantly related by their chemical structure to the neuroleptics. They are often effective against some of the muscular side-effects of neuroleptics and may be used for this reason. Chlorpheniramine ('Chlor-tripolon'), diphenhydramine ('Benadryl'), and promethazine ('Phenergan') are some of the more common ones. They are also sedatives and may be prescribed instead of regular hypnotics. Occasionally they are prescribed with neuroleptics to allergic individuals.

Antidepressants

There are many antidepressants. The most common ones are called *tricyclics*, because of their three-cycle chemical structure. They are thought to exert their action by controlling the brain chemicals known as noradrenaline and serotonin. The best known are imipramine ('Tofranil') and amitryptiline

('Elavil'). They are used for depression and may be used in schizophrenia when there is a secondary depression present. They have side-effects of their own and may add to the effects of neuroleptics and antiparkinsonians, so dosages of all three need to be carefully adjusted. Antidepressants take about ten days to three weeks to start working, so one must not expect depressive symptoms to respond right away. Doses often need to be raised in a gradual, step-wise fashion before the best effects are obtained. Sometimes two or three different antidepressants have to be tried before the right one is found.

Other medications

Other medications are sometimes used for individuals with special difficulties, and, of course, new agents are continually being developed. Do not hesitate to ask the doctor to explain the use of any medications with which you are not familiar. Amphetamines and related substances used in weight-reducing tablets are not advisable for schizophrenics. They may trigger symptoms of psychosis. It is important to make certain that *all* prescribing doctors know *all* the medications a person is taking, including *all* prescription drugs and *all* over-the-counter drugs. These include aspirins, nose drops, eye drops, contraceptive pills, allergy shots, vitamins, and such chemicals as caffeine (coffee, tea, chocolates, coca cola), alcohol, marijuana, and nicotine. Medication, especially in combination with other chemicals, can lead to drowsiness, so driving or exposure to dangerous machinery must be avoided until the drug schedule is well established.

FIVE

How relatives can help

Introduction

Relatives usually want to help the patient but feel helpless. They are not sure about the right way to help. Different authorities give them contradictory advice. When they get involved, they are told they are over-involved. When they back off, they are told they are uninterested. In fact, there is no *one* right way. A particular solution may work with one person at one time but not with another person or not with the same person the next time around. Much of what follows is advice rather than fool-proof prescription. Try one way, give it time, and see what happens. If it seems to be working, continue it. If it seems not to be working, try another tack. Speak to your relative's therapists – they may have some good suggestions. Above all, don't give up. Through much trial and error a workable solution will eventually be found.

When a person seems disturbed

Usually relatives have no idea what is wrong when a family member becomes ill with schizophrenia for the first time. If the person lives with the family, they may have noticed some strange behavior. Not knowing how to explain it, they may attribute it to a 'phase,' not unlike what they themselves or others in the family have experienced in the past. If the behavior continues to be decidedly 'odd,' the family will wonder about bad companions and drink or drugs. All sorts of explanations will be considered, the possibility of illness usually being left to the last.

Perhaps the first thing a family can do, then, is actively to consider mental illness when unexplained behavior transforms someone you love into a stranger. Information about different mental illnesses can be obtained from libraries, mental health associations, family doctors, psychiatrists, and psychiatric hospitals. Once mental illness is suspected, a number of steps can be taken.

The family must make every effort to speak with the individual concerned and to ask him what he thinks is happening. He may well be more worried and frightened than the family. He may already have recognized that something very puzzling has happened to his mind, to his emotions, and, it may seem to him, to the world.

The family should encourage him to see his family physician. General health problems can sometimes lead to the appearance of psychiatric symptoms. For example, disorders of the thyroid gland or of the adrenal gland frequently produce emotional disturbances. A full physical check-up is always indicated.

The family needs to consult long and seriously with the physician about the most likely diagnosis. The physician may not be sure and may suggest referral to a psychiatrist. This is not as ominous as it may sound at first. The psychiatrist may reassure the family that this is not schizophrenia. Or he may feel it is a mild form of the illness that can be treated in an outpatient setting.

Schizophrenia is a potentially serious condition and the diagnosis should not be made lightly. All concerned will want to ensure that it is correctly made. A period of hospitalization may therefore be essential for proper diagnosis. While an in-patient on a ward, a person enters into many relationships and is confronted with numerous tasks. During all of these, he reveals himself increasingly to those around him, especially to his doctor and nurse. This is the type of intensive assessment that is difficult to carry out on an outpatient basis. The patient will, predictably, not want admission. The family can be of great assistance by being informed and informative about hospital routines, reassuring, and consistently supportive of the decision (see chapter 2, on inpatient treatment).

When the patient is in hospital

Regular visits are usually appreciated and most psychiatric units have liberal visiting policies. Visiting may be restricted during meeting times, therapy hours, and meals. The ward staff will advise the patient and his family on what specific items might be needed for the stay in hospital.

The relatives are often the only people who can supply the important facts about what led up to the current symptoms, and their story is very important for diagnosis. The patient is often too frightened and perplexed to give a coherent story. Hospital staff ask the relatives to give their version of recent happenings to complement the patient's account. The following is an example of how essential it is for the psychiatric staff to interview the family:

The patient was a 20 year old male Portuguese immigrant. He entered the hospital terror-stricken and it was hard to obtain his story. It finally was learned that he had broken up with his girl-friend in the recent past and heard voices in his head saying he was a homosexual. The voices told him to visit a psychic in order to obtain a magic potion to cure him. He followed the instructions and consulted with the psychic but did not have enough money to pay her what she asked. Because of this she told him, he said, that she would follow him and kill him. The story sounded so bizarre and implausible and the man sounded so frightened and disorganized that a tentative diagnosis of schizophrenia was made. The auditory hallucinations seemed to bear it out.

When the family was interviewed with the help of an interpreter, they gave some very helpful background material. Apparently, they said, their son moped about for months after being rejected by his girlfriend. He was not interested in any other girls so his brothers and his friends, in order to 'get him out of it,' teased him about being a homosexual. Apparently this was a common tease in their community but their son was particularly sensitive to it because he was rather short and had always thought he looked 'too girlish.' In their community, it was the custom to visit psychics and obtain special potions, no matter what the ailment. The mother was herself in treatment by a psychic for 'rheumatism.' It was also true that psychics often charged very high fees, especially if they thought the ailment was of so embarrassing a nature that the client would not complain. Apparently, too, threats of revenge were not unheard of. In other words, all of the son's fears made sense in context. His emotions and behaviours no longer appeared to fit the diagnosis of schizophrenia. In fact he recovered very quickly, especially after his ex-girlfriend came to visit.

When the patient leaves hospital

After receiving a diagnosis of schizophrenia, both patient and family may feel deflated and hopeless. It is important for all concerned to realize that although there are serious implications, everyday functioning need not be interfered with in schizophrenia. One does not usually speak about 'cure' in schizophrenia, since symptoms do come back or may come back. One talks, instead, of 'social recovery,' meaning good functioning in all areas of life (educational, vocational, recreational, interpersonal) as long as treatment is continued. In this, schizophrenia is no different from many other medical conditions: diabetes, asthma, arthritis. When these illnesses strike in young adulthood, they disrupt many areas of functioning at first. With proper and ongoing treatment, the victim of schizophrenia is usually able to carry on with his life as before. Recovery, in some instances, however, may be slow and, in some instances, may be incomplete.

When recovery from schizophrenia is not complete, it may be difficult for the individual and for the family to accept limitations on what is possible. In the beginning, it may be very hard to give up long dreamed-of plans. A university education, for instance, may need to be abandoned. Marriage and a family may be unrealistic. The goal has to be self-sufficiency for the individual and that may mean a total turn-around in terms of previous vocational aspirations.

The most important thing a relative can do is to let the person concerned know that there is a future for him and that he, the relative, sees it as a rewarding future, far though it may be from what was originally hoped for.

This message can be conveyed in many ways. Talk to him and show an interest in what he is doing as part of his treatment program. Be enthusiastic about what he is doing even though at first it may sound dull and repetitious to you. Do not let your own standards on what is menial work and what is rewarding work erode your enthusiasm. Routine, predictable, non-stressful tasks are important for the schizophrenic to master first.

Should a schizophrenic be pushed?

Even before vocational mastery, the individual must become self-sufficient in terms of personal hygiene, food, and clothes. Relatives can help by expecting and encouraging him to master self-care tasks. How much to push depends on the particular stage of illness and also on what one is pressing the schizophrenic person to do.

When full social recovery has taken place and the condition is stable, the schizophrenic should be treated like any other family member. He should be expected to assume full responsibility for himself and he should take part in the duties of the household to the same degree as others.

When there are clear signs of continuing illness, the family must decide what is most important and what is less so. For instance, if he continues to have many active symptoms of schizophrenia then ensuring that he takes his medication regularly is more important than encouraging him to make his bed. Making sure that he attends treatment appointments has to come before visiting friends. Sometimes, in their zeal to have everything return to normal as quickly as possible, relatives expect too much too soon. It is usually more successful to decide what is crucial and make sure that *that* gets done. The rest can wait.

The most difficult time to decide whether to push or not is in the in-between stage when the individual is better than he was but not as well as he might be. Probably the easiest way to start is by expecting him to do the tasks he enjoys. That guarantees success and small successes increase enjoyment and feelings of self-worth. The household tasks that he dislikes can be left undone for the time being. It is best when the whole family agrees to this so that envy and jealousy do not develop. If the schizophrenic family member prefers putting out garbage to washing the dishes, he can forgo his turn at the dishes and make it up by an extra turn at the garbage. When you run out of enjoyable tasks, the next easiest to do are the simple routines. The convalescent schizophrenic patient is often too preoccupied to think things out. Giving him a long list of complicated instructions does not work. Ask him to do *one* thing. That done, he can be given the next instruction. Routines in terms of time, place, and accompanying person are more easy to follow than constantly changing demands. Do not hesitate to speak to him and to his therapist about what is appropriate as far as demands go and about what is too little, or too much.

When to leave the recovering schizophrenic alone at home

Everyone needs a break at times, especially if the home situation is tense and stressful. Individuals with schizophrenia will not always welcome the temporary departure of someone they care about, but that is not a reason to stay constantly at home.

It makes sense to stay at home when the schizophrenic is ill and not able to care for himself. When he is well and stable there is no reason not to go out for the evening, away for weekends, or away for a long vacation. The most difficult time to decide is when he is clearly not as ill as he was but is not yet fully himself. In many such cases, relatives stay at home because they feel too badly about leaving their charge to 'fend for himself.' A wiser move would be to prepare him well in advance; make the necessary arrangements for adequate supervision; inform relatives, neighbors, and the therapist; and go on vacation. It will be good for you and good practice for the schizophrenic in his pursuit of self-sufficiency.

If the recovering schizophrenic wants to take a holiday away from home, what then? The first such venture is very anxiety-provoking for the family. The best advice is to let him go. Try to help him make appropriate plans. Help him make contingency plans in case the original ones fall through. Stand by him whether the trip succeeds or not. Becoming self-sufficient involves trials and errors. The errors cannot be avoided. In fact, they are essential to eventual success.

Always make sure that adequate amounts of medication are taken along on the trip. For long absences, a statement from the doctor about the type and dose of medication should always accompany the patient. If the trip is to a sunny climate, make sure the patient has an appropriate sun-screen lotion (such as 'UVAL'). This lotion contains para-amino benzoic acid (PABA) and protects skin sensitized by neuroleptic medication against ultraviolet light. Broad-rimmed hats are also useful.

Should the schizophrenic socialize?

When an opportunity to socialize comes up, the individual should decide what he prefers to do about it. A big difficulty for relatives has to do with the schizophrenic's 'ambivalence.' This means that he frequently cannot make up his mind about what he prefers. Asked what he wants to do, he says one thing and then does another. This can drive the family to despair. It is important to remember that the schizophrenic is not doing this on purpose. He is literally unable to make up his mind. If this happens, the family has to be decisive. They can, for instance, flip a coin and then insist that the course of action be dictated by the results of the coin toss. They can call a family vote and insist that the majority vote decides. The patient is usually grateful if he is helped with decision-making in an impartial, non-autocratic manner.

Sometimes the schizophrenic family member wants to accompany the family on a visit but the others are reluctant to take him because of his potentially embarrassing behavior.

He may be afraid of eating in public or meeting new people, or he may experience perplexity or panic. Socially unacceptable behavior is likely to vary with anxiety. The more comfortable a person feels, the more likely he is to behave well. Try taking him first to close friends. Discuss with him afterwards any socially unacceptable behavior that occurs and try, together, to figure out how it could have been avoided. It is usually well worth it to experiment. Visits that promise to be embarrassing often turn out to be thoroughly enjoyable. There will, of course, be times when it will not be appropriate to take the patient. For example, a schizophrenic who has an overpowering fear of eating in public would make a poor guest at a banquet. The family's right and need for privacy must also be respected.

As the ex-patient gains confidence, he should be encouraged to plan his own entertainment. Re-contacting old friends can be an ordeal for many reasons. Frequently, the fact of a serious illness has destroyed what was once a close friendship. Patients may be more comfortable, at first, associating with new acquaintances whom they met in hospital. They share a bond of common experience that makes communication easier. Relatives often do not approve of these new friends who may be from the wrong social circle. It is important to remember that friendships present difficulties for schizophrenics and that all attempts at socialization should be encouraged.

How to treat the schizophrenic

When a person has socially recovered, he should be treated like anyone else in the family. Until then, allowances may have to be made. The schizophrenic, however, is not the only person in the family, and it is not realistic to treat him as if he were. The needs and feelings of other family members must also be considered. Social recovery can take some time. Until then, the schizophrenic may be preferentially treated. For example, he may be relieved of chores he is unable to do. This can be annoying to others, especially to brothers and sisters. It should be made clear in the family that, as soon as he improves, he will again be expected to 'pull his weight.' This situation is identical to any other where a family member suffers an illness, say a broken leg, and needs time to recuperate.

The danger is that the schizophrenic may grow to prefer his 'preferential status' to what he sees as the burdens and complexities of being well. He may decide that improvement is not worth it. This is a possibility with all illness, including broken legs. Some relatives worry about this possibility too much, some not enough. This is an issue that is very important to discuss with the individual involved, his therapist, and other family members.

Helping with sexual concerns

Some families are more open about sexuality than others. A tradition of openness is an advantage because a schizophrenic is often very preoccupied with sex. Some of his preoccupation as it occurs at the height of illness may be 'psychotic,' meaning unreal and somewhat bizarre. This means that he may read personal meanings into words and gestures. He may establish sexual rituals. He may bring up sexual topics at inappropriate times. Like any other active symptom in schizophrenia, this needs to be treated with understanding and patience, without disapproval, or shock, or censure.

On recovery, sexual matters should be handled as they are with the rest of the family. Sexual fantasies are usually private matters although relatives may find that the patient is more prone to discuss fantasy material than are other family members. It is helpful to realize that fantasy and reality are very different and that fantasy does not follow the same rules of right and wrong as does actual behavior. It is helpful to the patient to differentiate between fantasy and reality. Sensible questions about sexuality ought to be answered sensibly, strange questions by 'I really don't know about that, but your doctor might know.' Any concerns about the potential significance of sexual fantasies should be discussed with the individual and his therapist.

Masturbation (sexual self-stimulation) should never be a cause for concern unless it occurs excessively or in socially unacceptable situations. It sometimes makes the individual feel unduly guilty and this requires reassurance. Masturbation may be the result of the lack of appropriate interpersonal sexual outlets. However, the real concern may have more to do with the patient's worries over self-control. This is a common worry for schizophrenics: 'Am I in control of myself?' Nonjudgmental discussion of these issues is helpful and the concept of individual variations of sex drive can also be introduced in a supportive manner.

After social recovery, the schizophrenic will need encouragement to form partnerships with others whom he selects autonomously and responsibly. Intimacy is a problem for many; it may cause stress for recovering schizophrenic patients. It is hard for relatives to stand by and watch their son or daughter undergo such hardship at the hands, it may seem, of a cold, unfeeling other person. Difficult as these situations are, they are necessary, often ultimately rewarding. Relatives may feel pushed away and discarded during the patient's ventures into sexual relationships. Or they may unrealistically feel their job is over, that the individual has now formed closer ties. The reality is that there will probably need to be much experimentation, some successful, some not, before a satisfactory love relation is developed. The relatives can facilitate the experimentation, be sympathetic, and offer advice on responsible sexuality: contraception, sexual counseling, commitment to another person.

Helping a depressed patient

Symptoms of depression should never be taken lightly and are best reported to the doctor or therapist. Depression means feeling helpless and hopeless. Guilt and self-recrimination are usually part of it. So are listlessness, insomnia, lack of appetite, and lack of desire to do anything at all. Often this is accompanied by thoughts of suicide.

There is no magic answer to depression. Try to stand by and be patient. Do not blame a person for being depressed. He cannot help it. He may not be able to talk or to say what is on his mind. Do not expect him to. Be prepared to sit with him in silence. Try and say things and do things that will make him feel better about himself. Encourage exercise, good food, good sleeping habits, and socialization, but do not let yourself get frustrated if he balks at your suggestions. Do not let yourself get depressed, too. Depressed people are very draining. You will need time away from each other. Depressions, fortunately, are self-limiting. They do not last forever.

Helping an angry patient

Most of the time, anger is related to depression, unhappiness, and fear. Try to calm your relative's fears. Anger is often provoked by uncertainties or inconsistencies. Try to be clear and explicit and predictable. Try not to react angrily too readily.

Anger is a universal feeling, and, consequently, aggressive acts are common in all kinds of situations. Infants are born with a capacity for great rage and indeed the control of anger is part of the socialization process that we all go through. We all have internal conflict or external situations that lead us to angry feelings and often to fantasies of aggressive behavior.

Schizophrenia may have a significant impact on the occurrence of aggression within the family. There are some schizophrenics who become uninhibited when they are acutely psychotic. Occasionally, mothers with schizophrenia may become uninhibited and may abuse or neglect their children. During the illness, they may form a delusion of a paranoid nature involving ideas of revenge against others or the fantasy of needing to defend themselves against imminent attack. Sometimes patients may have auditory hallucinations that command them to violent acts. Of a similar nature are repeated thoughts to do with aggression though these rarely lead to action.

Generally, angry outbursts are reflections of the illness. The management is mainly medical. Comforting the patient with non-confronting remarks, food, or the opportunity of privacy may produce calmer attitudes. If necessary, the police may have to be called to get the patient to a doctor, but once the patient is at the hospital it is the responsibility of the physician to treat the basic disorder that led to the violent behavior.

Perhaps more common is the problem of hostility within the family when the patient is already in the recovery phase. The individual may be very frustrated by his illness, which he perceives as delaying the development of his life. He may hold the relatives responsible. The parents or spouse or indeed other members of the family may feel guilty about the patient's illness and also resentful of the demands that the sickness has placed upon them. At the same time, the patient is also feeling guilty and resentful. It is common to find in such situations mutual criticism and high levels of expressed emotion. This is an atmosphere in which aggression may arise and this may be not only from the patient towards the family members but from other family members towards the patient. If such episodes are recurrent, there is clearly a need for physical separation, time away from one another, and also for family counseling.

Helping with legal trouble

Sometimes poor judgment or psychotic thinking may lead to actions that produce a legal charge; by far the most are laid under traffic laws. Practice varies from community to community, but the crown attorney (Canada) or district attorney (United States) may be prepared to drop the charge or diminish the penalty if he is contacted directly by the relatives, if the nature of the schizophrenic illness is explained, if he is assured that the patient is under psychiatric treatment, and if he is assured that the family is available and strongly supportive. An up-to-date psychiatric assessment including diagnosis, severity, type of treatment, and prognosis (outlook) should be made available to the defence lawyer if the case is prosecuted.

Coping with death

Death of a family member or a close friend is an inescapable part of reality and a person with schizophrenia must face it as everyone else must. It is a major stress but the recovering schizophrenic cannot be shielded from it. It cannot be avoided or denied. If possible, the schizophrenic family member should be prepared for it by repeated family discussions.

The involvement of the schizophrenic individual in the events surrounding the death should be as full as possible. He has to be given a chance to say his last farewell like everyone else. At times of major family stress, such as illness and bereavement, the schizophrenic is often a tower of strength. It is as if reality, at those times, has finally impinged on his consciousness and has overpowered the mysterious and frightening fantasies that so frequently hold sway.

When the supporting relatives die

This is a concern relatives frequently mention. It is the best reason to encourage independent living for the ex-patient while the close family can still help. There are few schizo-phrenics who cannot learn to look after themselves or find their way about once their illness reaches a stable phase. Upon the death of the supporting relative there may be a momentary relapse, with readmission to hospital if necessary. Subsequent support from other relatives will usually be all that is needed. When this is not possible, life in a supervised residence may be the best alternative.

Is it better to live at home?

Families sometimes think it is better for their relative to be at home, but this may not be so. Individuals with schizophrenia usually do better in a home where there is not too much com-motion and where the general level of expressed feelings is low. But arguments, disagreements, and quarrels are part of family life. Some families try to avoid quarrels, to pretend disagreements never occur – this is not a good idea because it makes things unclear to the schizophrenic. He finds it hard to understand what is going on. However, loud voices and shouting matches are frightening and may provoke a return of symptoms in the patient, especially if minor criticisms lead to overwhelming accusations. An example of this is a request to make the bed which leads on to more sweeping statements about the patient 'never caring for those who love him.' Sometimes, life in a boarding home or a group home for ex-patients is more calm and involves less emotional pressure. In the long run, this may be to the schizophrenic's benefit.

It may happen that an ex-patient cannot manage to live on his own but refuses to move away from home to a boarding-house or supervised residence. And yet at home, he may be quite difficult to live with. It is very hard for families to ask a patient to leave, but having him at home may be very disrupt-ing to him and to the rest of the family, too. It is important to remember that a decision that the patient *not* live at home does not necessarily denote a lack of caring and is not an admission of failure. It may well be the wisest course of action. However, such important steps should always be taken in full consultation with the therapist so that appropriate back-up or 'rescue' plans can be instituted easily.

How much supervision?

The need for supervision varies. The extent of social recovery that the person has achieved and the amount of responsibility he can take on usually dictate the amount and the nature of supervision required.

For example, a person who has made a full social recovery is essentially on his own. He will need to keep on with his treatment but he will look after that himself and the family does not need constantly to check on him.

At certain stages of the illness, however, the family needs to make sure that the patient attends his treatment sessions, does not forget to take his medication, gets up on time in the morning to attend his classes, does not fight with others in the family, does not forget to shower and shave, and so on.

Unpredictable behavior and impulsive actions can occur in schizophrenia. For instance, the schizophrenic may suddenly decide to leave home or quit work, to get drunk or smoke pot, to yell at a neighbor or invite strangers into the house, to engage in irresponsible sexual behavior or attempt suicide. These are not everyday occurrences but they may happen, especially during periods of turmoil. It is not realistic to expect a parent or friend to anticipate and prevent all such occurrences. If something untoward does happen, do not jump to the conclusion that you are to blame, that closer supervision might have prevented it. Often individuals, including schizophrenics, learn only from their mistakes. Learning from experience is an important part of becoming self-sufficient. Speak

to the individual and his therapist about the amount of supervision that is required at various stages of illness.

What is 'over-involvement'?

When a schizophrenic patient is ill, he may be unable to par-
ticipate in discussions between his therapist and his family. At
these times, it may occasionally be simpler for the therapist to
talk with relatives alone. When the patient has recovered
enough to take part in the talks, most doctors or therapists
prefer that he be present. Ideally, there should be nothing
that needs to be said to the therapist that cannot be said in the
patient's presence. For the family to confide in the therapist in
private, with the request that the conversation be kept secret,
puts the therapist in a very uncomfortable position. Therapists will listen if you have something urgent to say, but will
tell the patient what they have learned from you. This is part
of the patient-therapist understanding.

The therapist-patient relationship and its confidentiality are
very important. Strictly speaking, the therapist cannot talk to
relatives about intimate details of the illness and treatment
without the patient's permission. This fact is difficult for relatives to understand, especially when they feel they have
something urgent to communicate. If a therapist, for whatever reason, ever refuses to answer a telephone call, write
him a note that lists all the important facts he needs to know.
Tell the patient you have done so.

Support of interested relatives is very valuable for the
schizophrenic. He may, however, not always accept this. He
may interpret interest and support as intrusiveness and 'med-
dling.' In that case, it is better to back off and stand by in case
of need, rather than to involve yourself actively. Ask your
relative's therapist for guidance in this, as it is a very important issue.

Money

Most schizophrenics are able to maintain control of their own finances. During difficult periods, there may be times when someone other than the patient should be looking after his financial affairs. If he is squandering his assets unwisely because of illness, the physician can make out a certificate of financial incompetence. This does not commit the patient to hospital, but legally turns his financial affairs over to another party, a private or a public trustee. This kind of overseeing of the patient's financial affairs may be necessary for short or sometimes for longer periods.

Relatives should consult with the family lawyer about the ins and outs of providing for the patient in their will. Large inheritances can be placed in investment securities and a monthly trust fund can be established for a disabled relative. It is wise to think ahead and reassuring to know that handicapped family members will be well looked after, no matter what happens to you.

Is schizophrenia a reason for divorce?

If the illness existed prior to marriage, the spouse knew what to expect and is usually more tolerant and accepting. If the illness arises after marriage, it is often very difficult for the spouse. Frequently the schizophrenic and his family blame the spouse, and the spouse ends up blaming himself or herself without cause. When there are small children in the family, this may provide extra strain and burden. A person suffering from schizophrenia may be unable to fulfil a parental role and the spouse may feel like a single parent, a wage-earner, and a nurse, all rolled into one. This may cause great resentment and may end in divorce. All love relationships are hard at times and there is no question but that schizophrenia can place very heavy burdens on marriages.

If the question of separation or divorce comes up, try to be very clear on what is making the situation intolerable. If it is illness-related behavior on the part of the schizophrenic, can that be eliminated by proper treatment? Will it be better in time? Try to sort this out with your spouse and his therapist. Is the problem a financial one? Is the individual's inability to earn a good living the problem? Is the problem his difficulty in being a parent, a lover, or an emotional support to you? How much of the problem has to do with your spouse's personality, quite apart from his illness? How much of the problem is the interaction between the two of you, again separate from schizophrenia? These are difficult questions to untangle. They will require discussions with your spouse, his family and friends, your family and friends, the therapist, a lawyer, and possibly a religious counselor. Try to talk with people who understand schizophrenia.

Can schizophrenics help relatives?

When an individual has recognized that he has a serious illness and that it is his responsibility to look after himself, the relatives' lot becomes much easier. Acceptance of illness is not easy and usually takes time. Once it has come about, the relatives can relax. Once the ex-patient has taken on the task of looking after his own well-being, he will make it his business to learn as much as possible about all aspects of schizophrenia and he will comply more or less enthusiastically with the treatment plan. At this point he now becomes a resource person for the relatives. The schizophrenic needs to ask questions about his disease, he needs to report all symptoms, he needs to talk freely to his therapist about his worries and concerns, he needs to be aware of the effects of his medication, and he needs to take pride in his strengths and accomplishments. Once he has taken on the full responsibility of maintaining his own health, the relatives become less tense and worried and, in turn, become easier to live with and enjoy.

How should relatives and friends respond?

People usually want to be as helpful as they can be to those in distress and so they look for the best ways to respond to a schizophrenic relative or friend. Perhaps it would be helpful to know that there is no best way and that sadness, anger, shame, and avoidance are natural ways in which individuals often respond to life crises.

This is true no matter what the crisis is. It is natural at first to ignore the problem, hoping it will go away. If it nevertheless persists, most people look for someone to blame. Pinning blame on ourselves or others, on God or on the government, seems to lessen the torment.

Nobody wants to blame the victim, in this case, the patient. Sparing him, however, can lead to suppressed rage and disappointment towards him and perhaps to unrealistic blame and undeserved anger directed towards others. While the patient is of course not responsible for the onset of his illness, he must, along with many others, take responsibility for his treatment and, ultimately, for his improvement.

Families and friends usually find that after the first shock and adaptation they begin to share the responsibility and begin to delegate the many tasks at hand. Some are tasks for the patient, some for the doctors and agencies, some for relatives. Some tasks are well accomplished but others fail and that may set in a fresh cycle of frustration and disappointment.

None of this response, of course, is specific to schizophrenia. Life crises of all kinds lead to chaotic emotions but they are also times of opportunity. It is important to realize that stress and unhappiness are to be expected and that most relatives will be able to cope without professional help. Many, however, find it helpful to share their feelings with someone who understands – for example, others in similar situations. If the emotional responses are difficult to bear, many find it helpful to seek help from a psychotherapist. The better the relative can come to terms with his own emotions, the more help he can be to the patient.

SIX

Support for relatives

Introduction

Schizophrenic illness presents family and friends with many crises. As with all crises, there are many individuals and agencies who would want to help. At times they do not know how to. Sometimes they try but give the wrong advice. Knowing the right person to turn to in a crisis is very important.

Help in case of 'relapse'

When symptoms have more or less disappeared, one speaks of *remission*. When symptoms reappear to a significant degree, one talks of *relapse*. Relapses are distressing for schizophrenics and relatives, though somewhat less so when anticipated and planned for. Schizophrenia, for the most part, is a 'relapsing' condition, and so it makes sense to expect a return of symptoms and not to be caught off guard.

It is best not to wait until the symptoms take on large proportions but to act early. The time to be worried is when the person first starts behaving in the way he did prior to his first illness. It is safe to assume that similar behavior means similar preoccupations, similar worries and concerns on his mind. The first step is to ask the person what is worrying him.

The next step is to suggest that the psychiatrist or the therapist be informed. If the person is reluctant to do so and you care for him, then tell him of your concern and tell him that you are going to contact his therapist.

If the therapist is unavailable, the best person to contact is the family doctor. In some communities, in an emergency, he can make a home visit. He may be able to evaluate the situation over the phone and make further recommendations or he may contact the hospital. A public health nurse or, in some communities, a mental health nurse, will also make a home visit. The earlier the situation is attended to the more likely the ill person's willingness to co-operate. Most hospital emergency departments are open twenty-four hours a day, seven days a week.

What to do if the individual refuses help

Try to find out why he is refusing. He may have a logical or an illogical reason. Sometimes he is afraid he will be hospitalized, or given a particular form of treatment he dislikes, or be attended by a particular person he dislikes. Sometimes it is possible to assure him that this will not be the case.

Often the individual has, by wishful thinking, convinced himself that he will never have a return of symptoms. The family, also by wishful thinking, has encouraged him to believe this. So when symptoms do return, it is tempting to deny them. Being prepared for the worst makes the worst not so bad. After an episode of schizophrenic illness, there is a 70 per cent risk of having a second episode within the year if the patient is not on medication. If the patient *is* on medication, this risk is reduced to 30 per cent. With very careful follow-up and intervention (temporarily raising the dose of medication or stepping up the frequency of appointments) subsequent hospitalizations can often be avoided. It is best to talk to your relative from time to time about the possibility of relapse and to plan together what should be done if that happens.

Often when the patient is adamantly refusing to see his therapist or denying that there is anything amiss, there may be one or two people who can get through to him. Among these one should consider other relatives, friends, employer or colleagues, minister, or, occasionally, fellow-patients.

Who can help?

Serious disturbance
If the patient is obviously very disturbed but continues absolutely to refuse psychiatric help, the family will have to acquaint themselves with the mental health laws in their community to see what can be done. Mental health law varies somewhat from state to state and province to province. The following measures are usually applicable:

1 Either the family physician or the treating psychiatrist can come to the house and, if necessary, can legally certify the patient as being mentally ill and in need of hospitalization. In some communities, the patient must be brought by the relatives to the evaluation service. Generally, involuntary hospitalization can take place only if, in addition to illness, there is the likelihood of the patient being harmful to himself or to others. That may mean that he is in great danger, for example, from hunger, physical illness, or self-neglect.

2 If the patient is threatening himself or other people, the police have to be called. Forewarn the police about the person's likely behavior and the reasons for it. Some communities have 'community officers' who are not uniformed. This may be less frightening to the patient and less upsetting to the family. Most specially trained officers, though not all, are very humane in their dealings with the mentally ill.

3 Because of unfamiliarity with their responsibility and liability in these circumstances, doctors or police may respond only in a limited way. This may be true in communities where mental health laws have undergone changes and nobody knows for sure what the new regulations are. The local psychiatric hospital or department of health information service can be contacted for information on the law and on appropriate procedures for ensuring the patient's safe conduct to a hospital. In some areas, the public health department will send a nurse to evaluate the situation if necessary. She may be able to persuade the patient to take medication on a doctor's order. Most mental health laws do not permit treating the patient, that is, giving medication, against his will, except under special circumstances. The nurse would know which doctor or which police officer to call to fill out the legal forms and escort the patient to hospital.

4 In communities where doctors are scarce or where the doctor cannot examine the patient, relatives may be allowed to give evidence under oath in front of a justice of the peace or magistrate to the effect that the patient is seriously ill and a risk to himself or to others. An order may then be issued to the police for the patient to be taken to the nearest hospital for an assessment.

5 Some hospital psychiatric departments have special teams that will come to the house in an emergency. They will assess the patient and suggest a treatment plan. In some cases, they will arrange for immediate hospitalization, even against the patient's will if they see evidence of serious mental illness and potential harm. Mental health legislation varies from country to country, state to state, and province to province. It always favours informal or voluntary hospital admissions, reserving involuntary hospitalization for those who are ill and at danger and unwilling to seek treatment.

Most mental health laws authorize the police to bring individuals to hospital for psychiatric assessment of several days' duration if they witness bizarre or dangerous behavior, or if they have a doctor's certificate to that effect, or if they have a judicial warrant. At the end of the assessment period, if there is sufficient cause, the individual may be kept in hospital for a further period, against his will if necessary.

6 Some families convince their ill relative by a show of numbers. In a demonstration of solidarity and strength, many family members together are able to obtain the patient's co-operation in going for treatment. Crises sometimes have this paradoxical capacity to bring the family unit closer and unite it in a common purpose.

Violence

Threats of violence and actual violence, including verbal abuse and attacks on property and persons, can occur when schizophrenics are agitated, deluded, and frightened. These can make the home atmosphere intolerable. A non-threatening approach to the patient is helpful. Try to remain calm and to avoid arguments and counter-attacks. An over-stimulating environment makes things worse. Try to reassure him of his safety and assure him that help is available. Families sometimes are embarrassed to involve others, but the presence of non-threatening friends or neighbors can defuse a difficult situation. Other people need simply be there; they do not need to interact or involve themselves with the patient. Make sure that the patient also has the opportunity for privacy, which may be essential for him. Do not hesitate to call for police assistance and state your case as strongly as possible.

Withdrawal

It is common for schizophrenics to become increasingly and painfully shy and withdrawn. This can be very frustrating to relatives who would sometimes rather provoke a spark of anger than be faced day-in and day-out with a wall of seeming indifference. It can be embarrassing in front of others to have your son or daughter or spouse hide in his room, or avoid looking people in the eye, or insist that you stay home with him. It is important to remember that such embarrassment is not necessarily a reason to spoil your own life and your relative's too. Friends and neighbors need not be avoided. The better they know the patient, the more comfortable they will be with him and he with them. Your life must go on and the schizophrenic family member will gradually adapt to your routines, your schedules, and your social and work life. In the long run, you are helping him to overcome his withdrawal by not capitulating to his demands for your constant protection. It is essential for your sake, and ultimately for his, that you live as full a life as possible.

Talk of suicide
Some schizophrenic patients can become quite depressed. These mood changes often reflect an understandable reaction to the illness. Vulnerable people may fear relapse and failure. They may blame themselves for their illness. The rate of suicide reported in most clinics for schizophrenia is considerably higher than that for the general population. Suicide usually does not occur at the very beginning of illness, when the individual involved does not really believe he is ill. And it does not usually come when he has come to terms with his illness. It is more frequent in the in-between stage, when the realization is new and not yet accepted.

Talk of suicide, no matter how vague, should be reported immediately. The reference to death is not always direct, but may consist of pessimistic or sad statements, such as 'What's the point?' Phone the hospital emergency at any hour. Ensure that the patient's therapist be informed and that he see the patient as soon as possible. Frequent personal contacts with the therapist are helpful. Hospitalization may or may not be necessary. Antidepressants may be prescribed or medications altered. Encouragement from relatives and friends often helps the patient to feel less of a disappointment and a burden to everyone.

If the patient does attempt suicide, relatives must try not to blame themselves. The person with schizophrenia is prone to many imaginings, with sudden changes not uncommon. He may misread and misinterpret events around him and experience acute depression. Knowing that this can happen takes away some of the anguish and self-blame. When a tragedy happens, it is human nature to look for someone to shoulder the blame: oneself, the doctor or therapist, friends. The apportioning of blame helps one to survive the pain and loss.

The treatment team

It is important to maintain regular contact with the treatment team. In most cases, relatives will be interviewed by a member of the team, and often by a social worker. The families' collaboration in providing additional information is essential for diagnosis, treatment, and planning for discharge. Some hospitalized patients might insist that their relatives not be contacted. This can place the treatment team in a quandary, because the patient's wishes have to be respected. In most instances, however, the family is kept informed and consulted prior to discharge. If you find that you are not contacted, take the initiative yourself.

It is your responsibility when speaking to the treatment team to ask direct questions. Do not hesitate to question the diagnosis, the treatment, the outlook, and so on. Do not hesitate to ask for a second opinion if you have any doubts. Try not to be discouraged by what is almost inescapable hospital routine: waiting, postponement, changing shifts, staff turnover, and one person sometimes contradicting what another has said. This last should not happen but often does. Most hospital personnel are well-intentioned but are often very busy and not always up-to-date on the latest team decisions. Do not be upset if you are asked not to visit for a period when your relative is very disturbed, but do keep in touch with the team.

Community resources

Schizophrenic patients are often involved with many helping agencies. These are described from the patient's point of view in chapter 3. Also see Appendixes I and II. Many of the same agencies have staff that, because they know the patient, can also be helpful to relatives. The community offers a variety of rehabilitation programs such as day treatment centres, vocational services, volunteer services, and self-help groups. In addition there are mental health agencies, public health nurses, community occupational therapists, and social workers. There are also family practitioners, general physicians, and psychiatrists. Do not hesitate to contact the local mental health division in your area for information.

Will there be more support for relatives?

Understanding and support for the families of schizophrenics will certainly increase in the coming years. The burden and responsibility of families have become clearer to mental health professionals over the last ten years.

Self-help programs initiated by relatives all over the world have been growing in popularity and have already produced extensive recommendations for improved health care (see Appendix II). As time goes on, there will be more emphasis on family strength – those forces that contribute to a more solid family unit and those factors that foster and develop coping mechanisms in each family member. There will also be increased efforts to educate the public about schizophrenia. There exists strong research evidence that relatives are not to blame – this information needs to be disseminated to the public at large.

One outcome of self-help programs will be the accumulated experience of relatives about what does and what does not work in the everyday interaction with schizophrenic relatives. There will be efforts to pool this large natural resource – the relatives – into effective and politically powerful organizations.

National organizations such as the National Alliance for the Mentally Ill, the National Schizophrenia Fellowship in the United Kingdom, and the Canadian Friends of Schizophrenics will grow. They are essential in helping to reduce the family's burden and in pointing out current gaps in the provision of mental health services.

SEVEN

Work and school

Back to school or work

It is quite feasible to return to school or work after an episode of schizophrenia although there is usually a period during which attention and concentration are not at the same level as they were prior to onset of the illness.

Quite often, ex-patients are ambivalent about returning to the work-force or have misgivings about returning to school after having lost a number of months of schooling. They often lack confidence in their ability to cope with their classes or jobs. It helps if the doctor, with the patient's permission, has kept the employer or teacher informed of the patient's progress. Vocational or scholastic assessments are useful to restore self-confidence. Some mental health centres have a teacher or vocational counselor on staff who may act as a consultant. It may be possible for the patient to train for work even before discharge from hospital. A temporary period in a sheltered and supervised setting may be beneficial.

Once working or in school, an employee or student is either competent or not. Medical diagnoses should not be an issue except when it comes to time off for medical treatment. Some employers and teachers, however, worry about someone with a diagnosis of schizophrenia. Much of the worry stems from not knowing what the term implies. We hope that this book will dispel much of the mystery. Problems will become less of a hindrance if employer or teacher and therapist can discuss them. Not all of the school- or work-related problems are found in every patient. As with other people, the start of a new job or class is often the critical point. Employers and teachers can help by structuring the situation early on.

Punctuality

Many individuals with a history of schizophrenia find it difficult to get up in the morning and face the day. Time pressures, crowded buses, and snarled traffic – universal problems – loom large. The result is that being late for morning work is not infrequent. Employees with a history of schizophrenia do best in jobs where the hours are flexible. They often prefer shift work, especially working those shifts when they are relatively alone.

Passivity

Employers and teachers sometimes complain that the person with schizophrenia shows relatively little initiative, or takes instructions passively, or shows little enthusiasm for the job. Some of the seeming passivity covers up anxiety and discomfort. When the person feels more comfortable, the real interest will start to show through. At any rate, not all jobs or studies require enthusiasm. Industry and reliability are usually more important.

Time off

For some schizophrenics long-term commitments are frightening. There may be a strong temptation to leave a new job or class and never come back because of fear and, sometimes, the conviction that no one will notice anyway, that no one will care. This is a very real problem for many people with schizophrenia and many potentially good jobs get sabotaged in this way. The understanding employer or teacher should telephone a person who misses work and express interest and concern. Once he knows he is missed and that his work really counts for something, the problem may be over.

Stress

The schizophrenic person does not handle stress particularly well. Highly stressful work with many deadlines and constant evaluation and competition is probably not the right kind. Schizophrenics tend to see people as more stressful than machines. The fewer people around, the better.

Clear instructions

People with schizophrenia are not good at reading between the lines. They tend to read *too much* between the lines, and to assume, when the message is not clear, that they are being criticized or put down. The message has to be very clear. Work instructions have to be simple and precise. One instruction at a time is easier to cope with than many given at once. Once a routine is established, everything becomes much easier.

Anger

People with schizophrenia get angry no more frequently or forcibly than anyone else. The only difference is that their anger is often unexpected and seemingly unprovoked. Because it seems to come out of nowhere, it is often difficult to cope with. Usually it is caused by reading something into what someone has said or misinterpreting something someone has done. It can be avoided or quickly quelled if the person explains what it is that was said or done and what was intended.

Moodiness

If a schizophrenic's moods seem very changeable and there is much irritability, it may be a sign of the return of active symptoms. It helps if the teacher or employer has the kind of relationship with the employee or student where this type of problem can be openly discussed and a recommendation to get in touch with the therapist can be made. Frankness is to be preferred over complaints about the employee to others.

Slowness

Teachers or employers may notice slowness on the part of schizophrenic students or employees and wonder if this is caused by the medication used to treat schizophrenia. In some instances the slowness may be due to medication; in other instances it may be a result of preoccupation. If the job requires speedy work and the person is incapable of it, it may be best to suggest a different job rather than to demand the impossible.

Isolation

A preference for being alone should not unduly worry the employer or teacher. Often the schizophrenic person does better work when he is by himself and away from interpersonal stress.

Preoccupation

Preoccupation may be a sign of worry about doing the job well. It may, however, signal problems. If this worries the employer or teacher he must feel free to approach the employee and ask him about it.

Appointments with a therapist

It is very important that the student or employee be able to continue his regular appointments for medication and counseling. Some doctors and clinics have evening hours, but many do not. Allowing regular time for appointments, even if it means missing time from work or school, safeguards the employee's or the student's health and his work.

It is often helpful if the employer or teacher, with the schizophrenic's consent, has an opportunity to talk to the therapist. In some instances, particularly early on in the employment or school year, it might be possible to arrange for an on-the-spot visit by the therapist.

Special settings

Many schizophrenics are never able to enter the competitive work-force, and for these people there exist in most communities sheltered work settings and special vocational placements. These may be required temporarily, for a training and adjustment period, or for prolonged periods. Pay is a problem since a person working a full day deserves at least a minimum wage, and special programs are unable to provide this.

Conclusion

Those persons with a history of schizophrenia who *are* able to work competitively usually become loyal, reliable, indispensable employees.

EIGHT

The future

Changing public attitudes

Attitudes towards schizophrenia have changed to a considerable degree. Since the 1950s, particularly since the introduction of effective drug treatment in 1952, more and more schizophrenics live in the community rather than in psychiatric hospitals. This change has allowed the public to come into contact with recovered patients. More and more people have come to realize that there is no reason to be frightened of schizophrenia. Not everyone, however, has been fortunate enough to have had first-hand contact with recovered patients. Many people still live in fear of schizophrenia, imagining the sufferer to possess two unpredictable personalities, a Mr Jekyll and a Dr Hyde.

Such a view cannot persist much longer, because it is so very far from the truth. There has been continuing education about schizophrenia, and the more this continues, the faster public attitudes will change. The stigma attached to mental illness as a whole, though still present, is not as pronounced as it was. More and more relatives and ex-patients are speaking openly about schizophrenia. This will, undoubtedly, become a powerful force in changing public opinion.

More facilities

Hospitals, rehabilitation centres, and community support systems already exist. Some areas have more facilities than others, usually because a local pressure group of interested persons was able to stimulate interest, change local bylaws, and garner funds. Interested, knowledgeable, and highly motivated groups of people are the keys to improving present supports and developing new ones. For example, in most communities, there continues to be an unmet need for supervised group homes or apartments for those schizophrenics who have no family or who cannot live with their family. An organized group of interested non-professionals working together could do much towards developing such facilities. The same applies to the need for social and vocational programs.

As new, still experimental programs for rehabilitation prove successful, there will be a need to expand them so that all schizophrenic patients can reap the same benefits. Staying abreast of new developments in the treatment of schizophrenia and working together politically to make sure that successful treatment strategies are implemented in local communities are challenging and eminently worthwhile tasks for relatives. (See Appendix II for existing relatives' groups.) Pressure on government must emphasize the need for equitable funding for community-based programs.

Will there be a cure?

Cure means complete eradication of problems with no need for further treatment. There is no cure for schizophrenia. There is no cure at present for many medical disorders. Practically all illnesses other than short-term infections require continuous monitoring to ensure that symptoms do not reappear. So it is for schizophrenia. In the future, when the exact cause of illnesses, including schizophrenia, is better understood, the chances of finding a cure will improve.

When most people ask about cure, however, they are thinking about control. They want to know, 'Will he get over his present problems and will he be able to resume a place in society?' The answer to this question, in most cases is yes, although perhaps a qualified yes.

Forty years ago schizophrenic symptoms were so difficult to manage that two-thirds of individuals admitted to hospital for schizophrenia stayed there upwards of two years. Ten years ago, after effective drugs had been around for twenty years, only one in ten patients needed a hospitalization of two years' duration. Today it is rare for patients to stay in hospital longer than ninety days. That is because of more effective medications and more widespread community supports for the convalescing patient.

If one looks at other indications of improvement (freedom from symptoms, employment record, interpersonal involvement, personal satisfaction, family's satisfaction), 80 per cent of people with schizophrenia do well. With more research and better treatment, that percentage will increase and the extent of improvement will broaden.

Current research

There is much excitement and activity in schizophrenia research currently. One or two neurotransmitter substances (brain chemicals) have been known and studied for a long time. The last few years have brought to light many previously unknown brain transmitters that all interact in a complex manner. Some disarray of these chemical substances is probably responsible for many of the symptoms of schizophrenia. The names of some of these neurotransmitters are dopamine, serotonin, endorphins, GABA, acetylcholine, and substance P. Not only do they interact with one another but they are also affected by a multitude of enzymes and peptides (protein substances) in the brain. Some of these enzymes make easier and some make more difficult the action of the neurotransmitters at specific protein sites (receptors) on the membranes of nerve cells in the brain.

It is impossible of course, to study the brain cells directly. One can, though, study the action of these chemicals on other cells taken from a schizophrenic patient. All the cells in the body, including blood cells, are related and have certain properties in common with nerve cells. Alternatively, one can study animal brain cells, although, of course, animals do not develop schizophrenia. One can also make post-mortem studies of brain regions of schizophrenic patients who have died. It seems that specific post-mortem brain regions of these people contain more dopamine receptors than the same regions in the brains of non-schizophrenic individuals. This is an important finding. It may be partly a result of neuroleptic treatment. Or it may result from years of specific symptoms. It may even have been present from birth. New X-ray techniques (CT scans) have revealed areas of shrinkage in the brains of some schizophrenic patients. It is not known if these irregularities produce the symptoms of schizophrenia or if they are a reaction to the illness. Still newer techniques (PET scanning) reveal not only brain structure but also brain functioning.

Besides this burgeoning field of physiological, radiological, and biochemical research, studies continue on attempts at uncovering the patterns of hereditary transmission of the disease. More work is being done on making the diagnosis more accurate and objective and on specifying the trigger factors that precipitate illness. Better and more efficient treatments are being studied. There are now ways of determining by a blood test whether the patient is absorbing his medication and whether the dose is adequate. Drug companies are trying to make new drugs with fewer side-effects. Community and social programs are being studied for long-term effectiveness in preventing illness and in improving the quality of life for individuals with schizophrenia.

Easy-to-understand publications such as *Science News*, *Discover*, *Omni*, and *Science Digest* frequently feature stories on recent advances in this field.

PART TWO
Personal accounts

NINE

A mother's account

About five years ago, at the age of twenty-four, our daughter became very disturbed: she was hearing voices, felt she was being followed, and her days and nights were filled with constant fear and anguish. Her father and I were puzzled and distraught. A few months later, Elizabeth was admitted to hospital.

Though her father and I visited her each day of her four-month stay, we remained perplexed by her illness. During the entire period we never met her doctor. *We* had not asked for an appointment with him, and *he* had not requested to see us. Just prior to her discharge, we had an interview with the social worker who briefly outlined some useful tips to help Elizabeth get established back home with us. She warned us to watch for certain danger signs that would indicate recurring illness. Plans would be made for Elizabeth to attend a sheltered workshop and she would visit her own doctor on a regular basis to have her medication supervised.

The interview appeared over, but I had an important question. 'What was the diagnosis?,' I asked. The answer was a blow! Our daughter was schizophrenic. We asked whether we should tell our relatives and friends. Should we tell Elizabeth?

Should we keep it a secret? 'What kind of life lies ahead for our daughter? Will she be able to go back to school? What about boyfriends and marriage?' we wondered aloud. Most of these questions were not comprehensively answered. However, we were advised to keep the nature of the illness to ourselves. Elizabeth was not to be informed about the diagnosis yet. At my insistence, she would become an outpatient at the same hospital and visit her psychiatrist for a brief interview whenever she needed a new prescription. If there was a chance of repeated illness, I certainly wanted a psychiatrist to be seeing her. And so, virtually uninformed and totally mystified, we brought Elizabeth home to live with us and to a job at a sheltered workshop.

To our surprise, we found Elizabeth much easier to live with than she had ever been before. Like an obedient child, compliant and dependent, she carried out all orders, took her medication regularly, and was conscientious about her duties at the workshop. We looked after her, not expecting her to contribute much to the work around the house.

But living with Elizabeth was like living with a robot and we became increasingly concerned. We looked for an explanation of her condition and blamed both the shock therapy and the medication. Perhaps if the medication were reduced she would be less sluggish, less childlike, we thought. We were, however, in a dilemma, since we did not want the drugs decreased at the risk of her illness returning.

Our younger daughter begged us to make an appointment with the psychiatrist. We agreed with her that we should find out the long-term implications of her sister's behavior. We had important questions: Could the medication be reduced? Was there an alternative to the sheltered workshop? Was there a group home that she might eventually move into?

Unfortunately, the meeting between Elizabeth's doctor and my husband turned out to be a great disappointment.

Elizabeth was on a mere maintenance dose that could not be reduced further and it was best for her to continue at the workshop and to live with us, he advised. The implication was that the situation was not likely to improve ever, and for the first time we felt despair about the future.

However two or three things happened about this same time that brought dramatic changes to Elizabeth's life.

First, our younger daughter Pamela and her little girl came to live with us, filling our house with activity and giving Elizabeth other young people to mix with and some baby-sitting responsibility. Furthermore, Pamela chided us once more about our complacency. She felt Elizabeth needed a more stimulating atmosphere to live in. We were treating her like a retarded person and keeping her too dependent. She sensed that Elizabeth was at a stand-still at the workshop. She made arrangements with her father to have Elizabeth work in his office and trained her in the evenings to do jobs that she could easily manage. She urged us to see another psychiatrist to have a second opinion about Elizabeth's potential for a more independent life.

The second significant occurrence was the change of Elizabeth's doctor. The new psychiatrist was an immediate hit and we were delighted when he invited us to have an interview with him to discuss Elizabeth's progress and to ask questions and make suggestions. Two years after Elizabeth's discharge from the hospital we went back for a meeting with him and a psychiatric nurse. It was a marvelous encounter, with warm, concerned, and understanding professionals. We were immensely excited and optimistic!

That momentous meeting generated a number of changes in our lives, which in turn contributed to a marked improvement in Elizabeth's behavior. Among other things, Elizabeth became enrolled in a special clinic and my husband and I joined a relatives' group. I must emphasize how beneficial both these connections have been and continue to be for all of us.

Gradually there was a tremendous change in Elizabeth. She began to walk down the street faster, she became more interested in her personal appearance, she began to help around the house, and she went out more. It was as though she were coming back to life.

Last summer she took a trip to Venezuela to visit a former high school friend and her husband. We were worried about the trip and the change in eating and sleeping patterns, but we had to let her go! She had planned the trip and saved the money for it totally on her own. She had an exciting time and arrived home in great shape.

This last year has brought further change. Less compliant, more self-assured, she is ready to challenge us and to argue and stand up for her rights. Just recently a friend of ours who had not seen Elizabeth for a year remarked on the unbelievable change. She commented on her composure, her liveliness, and her contribution to the conversation.

The spectacular change in our daughter was not the result of medication change. Undoubtedly, it was tied in with good professional help and with a more stimulating atmosphere at work and at home.

However, after five years, there still remains the challenge of trying to help Elizabeth become much more independent. She cannot really do that while she works for her father and lives with us. She is now beginning to ask about other jobs and about the necessary training for them. We are exploring the possibilities of a group home. With the support of the clinic and of the relatives' group, we think these goals can be accomplished. We are optimistic about Elizabeth's future.

TEN

A father's account

My daughter called from Ottawa, Ontario, one day to say, 'Please send money.' She had gone on a two-day trip and taken $200. We couldn't see that she would need more. 'It's very important,' she said, 'a very important person is interested in me.' This sounded odd but, at first, believable. That was the main problem when she first started getting sick: we didn't know if it was make-believe, if she was teasing us, if she was angry at us, or if she was just confused. We quickly realized that it was no fun for her. Her so-called adventures with movie stars and Hollywood producers and politicians and royalty were not making her happy and left her upset all the time. Was she under too much stress at school? we wondered. Was I as a parent responsible for this upset in my child and if so, in what way? How could I help her face up to reality and accept responsibility for her increasingly inappropriate behavior? Not knowing what to do, we tried to write it off as a passing phase, something she would outgrow, and we did nothing.

As reasoning with her became more and more impossible, it all became too much to cope with – for her and for me, too.

Finally, at the end of our patience, we had to turn to professionals for help but it took us *five years* to realize she had an illness!

Then we were told she had to go to a hospital. This was incredibly upsetting to us, but we had no choice. Her behavior was impossible to control by then. She had dropped out of school, wouldn't look for work, stayed in bed all day, went out at night, and came back with these extraordinary stories. When she was in hospital there was an initial sense of relief that she might now get the help she needed. Then came the shock: We were told that the diagnosis was schizophrenia. They tried to explain what that meant, but it's not an easy thing for a parent to grasp. The main treatment recommended seemed to be drug therapy and we were against that somehow. We didn't know much about schizophrenia then.

I think we weren't alone in having unrealistic expectations about what psychiatry could do and how our child should be treated. I think professionals don't spend nearly enough time explaining, reassuring, and supporting parents. Much of what we learned came by guesswork.

Education of parents and family members about schizophrenia is crucial. Meeting other relatives in a similar position as ourselves is also needed. We found we had to go after assistance, keeping our ears tuned to all sources. Nobody thought to refer us for this kind of help.

Our daughter's problems are not gone. But we are much better informed and know better how to cope with situations as they arise. When she says Prince Charles is courting her, we know it isn't an attention-getting device or a piece of silliness or a maneuver to get more money from us or a deliberate ploy to drive us crazy. That's what we used to think. We realize now that that is how her mind works. When she's feeling down she will try anything to get her spirits up, I think.

Now when she says Prince Charles is interested in her, we don't quarrel with her. We don't avoid her either, as we had started to do when we thought she was crazy. We tell her *we're* interested in her and we make little attempts to make her feel better about herself. It seems to work.

ELEVEN

I am a schizophrenic

My name is Sandra. I was diagnosed as a schizophrenic eleven years ago, at the age of twenty-five. Until then I had danced professionally in various nightclubs and, at one point, taught ballet.

In the course of my illness, I went from being a dancer pursued by millionaires and movie stars, to a divorcee working part-time selling two-dollar earrings, and then on to welfare, before I was able to start picking myself up again.

I am now, thanks to treatment and support, a psychiatric nurse, helping people diagnosed as I am, and many others as well. I graduated from nursing three years ago, standing first in my class, with an overall average of 86 per cent.

You will notice the title I have given this chapter is 'I *am* a schizophrenic' and not I *was* a schizophrenic. Like an alcoholic who has to stand up at a meeting of Alcoholics Anonymous and admit 'I *am* an alcoholic,' so I have come to regard schizophrenia as something that is always with me, although not always in a troublesome way.

I would like to take this opportunity to discuss the feelings one experiences in coming to terms with schizophrenia and show how psychiatry has helped me, in the hope that many will realize that they are not alone, and that when you're 'down' the only way is 'up'!

Understanding schizophrenia

It is not easy to understand an illness like schizophrenia that brings you to a psychiatric facility for help. We are quite prepared to accept the fact we may have a sore arm or aching leg, but how does one accept the fact they have a 'sore' head? For the older set, there was a movie, *Snake Pit*, which portrayed Olivia de Havilland locked up, with the key thrown away. Or for the younger set, *One Flew Over the Cuckoo's Nest* brought a new sort of fear – lobotomies and shock treatments.

The illness makes us enter a new world, with the possibility of our clothes being taken away from us, or the door being locked for a time to detain us. In most cases we do not realize that it is for our own protection.

We are faced with fears. 'I'm scared for I've never experienced anything like this.'

Some of us feel relieved. 'Home was such hell; this place is like heaven; it's no hassle.'

There are feelings about prior hospitalizations such as 'I feel like a failure when I have to come here. To enter the hospital every few years is something I can't cope with. When I come back, I know I haven't made it.' Or thoughts like, 'I spent six months on a violent ward. I remember another patient slugging me. It was scary, and I thought this place might be the same way.'

Yes, all these thoughts are a hindrance in understanding our illness.

Then there is medication. How does one accept the necessity of having to take medication for a long time, especially when it can make you feel unable to think, or shaky and nervous, or like pacing up and down endlessly.

And to add insult to injury, we are told 'You are schizo-phrenic.' How does one accept this when one has seen the movie *Three Faces of Eve*? I don't know about Joanne Wood-ward, but I have always had only one personality, although when I was first told that I was a schizophrenic, you can bet your life I spent a lot of idle time trying to find my other personalities.

Yes, we all have fears, some real and some imaginary, and they take time to disappear.

And what about the stigma of being in a psychiatric facility? 'Are my friends going to find out?' 'Is my boss going to find out?' 'If I tell anybody where I was, they might think I'm crazy.'

This brings on another fear: 'I must be "crazy," or why would I be here?'

So, how does one understand? Well, by talking about how we feel and by asking, reading, discussing with others, and by comparing experiences.

Because of the fears, it took me a long time to understand my illness. I never read, thought no one could possibly un-derstand how I felt, especially the nurses and doctors, for they have never been through this. But through reassurance, com-fort, and talking, I realized that there are a lot of people who do understand. Even though maybe they haven't been through the actual illness, they have all been through some traumatic experiences.

Accepting the illness

During my ninth hospitalization (this by itself should tell you how long it took me to accept my illness), I remember writing a poem about the ward I was on. I was very proud of myself, as it was put on the bulletin board for everyone to read. I do not remember the poem any more; however, one line really sticks out in my memory: 'I'm not crazy – they are,' referring to my friends around me. How I denied the fact that I needed help!

Denial is perhaps the worst phase of this illness to go through, and the most costly in time. My average length of stay in hospital was six to eight weeks and I was hospitalized nine times. I thus wasted a year and a half of my life denying the fact I was schizophrenic. How did I do it?: by going off medication as soon as I felt well. How I hated that medication! Every time I took it it was a constant reminder that something was wrong with me, and I hated to think that something was wrong with me.

Everytime I was hospitalized, I was told the same thing: 'If you stay on the medication, and see your therapist, you probably wouldn't have to be in hospital.' But how I hated to take that medication!

I started to ponder this on my last admission. 'The medication must work. It gets me well enough to get out of here.' 'Do I want to keep on being hospitalized the rest of my life?' 'Maybe I should stay on the medication, I'm not sick, however, it must do something.'

During my last stay in hospital, I was made to confront my denial. I came to accept the fact, through much psychotherapy, that I was schizophrenic, and during my last week in hospital, I was one of three people chosen to talk to over 200 medical students. I remember getting up on that stage and the doctor who was conducting the seminar asking 'Sandra, what is your problem?' I promptly answered, 'I am schizophrenic.' It didn't hurt. In fact I was proud, as I had come to terms with my illness. Five years later, nursing school, a nursing career – it still doesn't hurt.

Friends and relatives

It has been my experience that friends and relatives come in four varieties:

The indifferent ones (or the 'duty' ones)

These are the ones who come to bring you cigarettes when you're in hospital, ask you how you feel, and go on to discuss their own problems. (They do the same when you're not in hospital.)

This hurts. If any one needs comfort and reassurance, it's us. We're going through hell, you know. Try to understand what's happening to us. We feel weak, vulnerable, and very mixed up. Don't think just because we're safe in the hospital it's over – it's not. We have to wrestle with every feeling, thought, and emotion we are feeling; and it's not easy.

The overprotective ones

These are the ones who see us as 'invalids.' We can't do anything any more. We should just stay home, rest, and be babied. Quit school, give up our jobs, et cetera. *Don't*, please don't do this. Accept the fact we're a little helpless now but not hopeless.

I remember speaking to a group of schizophrenics who were meeting with their parents. One of the parents was fearful about taking his daughter on a six-week trip to Europe. 'It would be too much of a strain.' I was furious! Don't make us feel any worse! Encourage activities we were once doing. If you don't accept us, who will?

The fearful type

'Well, he's crazy now, better stay away from him.' This hurts. How do you expect us to get well if you won't accept we are ill and can get better with help? It makes *us* deny we are ill even more, and it's very lonely, being 'alone.'

The honest type

They are at first as bewildered as the other types but they are obviously trying to learn about the illness, both from us and from others. They are constantly looking for answers to problems and questions, both on their own as well as with us.

Hospitalization (The team)

I remember one of my most frustrating concerns as a patient: 'How can I expect to get well when I never see the doctor?' Like every other patient my doctor knew everything, no one else did, and he, and he alone, could help. I never understood the importance of psychologists, social workers, occupational therapists, or nurses. I only wanted to see my doctor, and could never understand why he wasn't at my beck and call.

Now that I am a nurse, I would like to introduce you to 'The Team,' with the doctor as head of the team. Why a team? The doctor has many patients and cannot spend all his time with you. So all the members of his team act as mini-doctors by listening to you, helping you grasp your problems, and guiding you towards a solution to your problems. As team members we all write notes or inform the doctor in person of how you are doing, and he makes the decisions as a result of the team's effort to help you. So do not feel you are being ignored. Many are working for you. And many are much more approachable and understanding and helpful than the doctor.

Boring the therapist

As a patient and as a nurse, I have come to realize there is no such thing in psychiatry as boring the therapist. Everything one says helps the therapist understand what the patient is all about. And by helping them realize what we are all about, they can in turn help *us* realize what it is that bothers us about ourselves. Take my own case as an example.

I see my psychiatrist on the average every two weeks or once a month. In examining what I am 'all about,' it became clear that many of my symptoms crop up when I am rejected by members of the opposite sex. My doctor and I now spend our therapy sessions mainly discussing the men I know and how I react to them. I used to feel I was wasting her time talking about things that I thought would be better discussed with a girlfriend, but I have realized that this is part of the treatment that keeps me well.

It is very important to take responsibility for raising problems and for working at one's difficulties. Being honest and direct with therapists helps a great deal.

Expecting the world to look after you

As I explained earlier, I went from being a dancer pursued by millionaires and movie stars to a divorcee selling two-dollar earrings, and then to being on welfare. Part of the reason for my difficulties was that I felt sorry for myself. 'Why am I sick? Why am I always in hospital? Why aren't my friends in hospital? Why aren't my family?' Expecting the world to look after you is again a form of DENIAL. It is denying the fact that we feel alone, helpless, and hopeless, that we need help, that we're sick, and many other things.

Don't let this happen to you. TALK ABOUT how you feel. DON'T REMAIN ALONE. Join activities, see your doctor or therapist, tell them how you feel. Again, don't feel nobody understands, they do. It is natural to feel sorry for yourself at one point, but don't stay 'down.' Being 'down' is degrading financially, physically, and emotionally. Feeling helpless makes one feel hopeless; having hope brings help. The medical profession will always offer help even if friends and relatives don't, so accept it.

Don't give up!

I recall how I was starting to give up. Looking back now I can genuinely say that it was my own fault. I NEVER UNDERSTOOD the fact that help was there. I kept thwarting it by not accepting that the medical profession knew more than I. 'No one could possibly know or understand what I was going through.' I never understood that I was denying the illness that for several years brought me so much misery, I never understood that I was not capable of coping with many problems on my own. I never appreciated that many of my hospitalizations were my own fault. In other words, I never understood MYSELF, and half the battle in getting well is getting to know yourself.

So, get to know yourself! Get to know that most of the emotions we feel are normal and that we all have problems and have to learn to talk about them and to understand them, and then to cope with them.

TWELVE

A schizophrenic's story

Have you ever woken up realizing that something is seriously wrong and you don't know if it is physical or mental?

Well this happened to me. I thought that I was going to have a heart attack: the pounding in my chest was ceaseless, my head was spinning. I couldn't think or do anything. All I could do was lie there and suffer. This was the beginning of my breakdown, brought about by several things. A workaholic, worrying all the time, I was slowly losing touch with reality, preferring instead to daydream all the time.

I phoned a psychiatrist, whom I had seen a few times the year before. I tried, through screaming and crying, to explain that something had definitely gone wrong with me over the past year. He recommended that I come to the hospital. I agreed and that became one of several admissions to a psychiatric ward.

Immediately after being admitted, the relief that flowed through my veins slowly relaxed my mind, but I also went back to my fantasy world. I was psychotic, but it was the rest of the world that was at fault. I fooled everyone except myself. On discharge I took a vacation in California. The whole time I was away I couldn't face the reality of having been psychotic. More and more I would retreat, to the living hell in my mind. I was feeling terribly guilty about everything I had thought and done for twenty years. I was talking to myself and crying and laughing all at the same time. I was thinking that the only way out of this hell was to be violent, not only to myself but to those around me too. I hated myself and my loved ones, but most of all I hated the world. I became increasingly listless and withdrawn, locking myself in my room for days at a time. I had to make a decision: either kill myself or hurt someone or get help. I decided to get help.

I went on day care this time. I was taking 'Valium' and 'Stelazine' just to be able to get up in the morning, but when my psychiatrist took me off 'Valium' I went through hell for two weeks: convulsions, vomiting, diarrhea, and no appetite at all. Other tranquilizers and antidepressants did not help. The doctor couldn't figure out what was wrong. He guessed that I might have a form of schizophrenia but he didn't tell me. Instead he transferred me to a psychiatric hospital for the more intensive care I needed. My new doctor told me that he was not yet sure of the diagnosis, but that I was very sick. When he stopped all medication, I felt angry. I wasn't sleeping, and I was hallucinating. While lying on one bed I could actually *see* myself getting up out of another bed. I was hearing strange people whispering words into my ears. My doctor then told me that I had a form of schizophrenia. He put me on increasing doses of chlorpromazine. It slowed my thinking down and had a calming effect, but it didn't take away my violent thoughts. I realized that it was time for me to face the reality of my situation and start to deal with it. I couldn't just sit there with my thoughts and expect the staff and drugs to cure me. That is only 10 per cent of it. What people with mental illness must first realize is that most of the cure or control of mental illness is up to the patient. If you want to get better badly enough, you will. The longer you sit and do nothing, the longer it will take to get better. In fact, you may get worse. At first I didn't believe it, but deep down inside, I had the desire and motivation to better myself. What I needed was a spark to get going. In my case they used reverse psychology, which caused me to rely less and less upon feeling sorry for myself and more and more in both co-operating (not conforming) with the staff and listening to how other patients felt and talked. Soon I realized that I wasn't as badly off as I had thought. There were other patients who didn't have a friend or family to speak to. I found myself wanting to talk to them more and more. This was a new beginning for me. I was finally listening to what someone else had to say. I had not cried for a whole year until then. I was still having problems with not being able to think straight.

A change of medication did not help me to straighten it out. This is when I began electroconvulsive therapy (ECT). The first one, of a total of eighteen, gave me a headache. I received these treatments Monday, Wednesday, and Friday morning, over a period of six weeks. Although I had thought of it as a rather grisly form of treatment, it actually worked on me. It slowed my thinking down to normal speed and, together with a drug called pericyazine ('Neuleptil'), actually helped me to reorganize my unsorted mind.

The next step was psychotherapy. This was a heated and mind-blowing experience. My doctor was basically trying to help me help myself, but I continued to have violent thoughts to the point of being afraid to light a cigarette for fear of setting the ward on fire. Despite those periods of irrationality I was slowly regaining stability and strength. One day finally my defensive wall came down. I was so angry and upset I wanted to both hit my doctor and break down and cry. I did the latter:

it was my first relief in more than a year. Rather than accepting my anger early on, I used to deny to the end that I was angry at anyone.

The next week my doctor informed me that I would be discharged in three weeks. With no place to live and no future to speak of, I felt I had to do something to enable me to stay on in hospital. The old anxiety returned, my head was aching, and the violent thoughts became stronger and I started to withdraw again. I pleaded that I was still crazy and a danger to myself.

My social worker whom I still love as I love my family gave me a tremendous amount of support. She explained to me about life in a group home, which is a home where people who have had emotional and mental problems live together and share day-to-day problems. There are also problems that arise as the result of living with ten other people under the same roof. The fact that some may still be slightly ill can be depressing to someone who is trying to climb the ladder of accomplishment again. It is a reminder of one's immediate past. The good thing about it is that it pushes you to try harder to help yourself.

My social worker helped me find a group home two weeks before discharge. We went there during the evening and were welcomed very warmly. I thought to myself that maybe this is the place to make another start in life.

In the hospital I had just completed the program in rehabilitation testing. The tests showed that I was intelligent and could be whatever I wanted to be. They asked me if I would like to take a college course in job-readiness training. I was terrified at first. I would fail and become a lost cause. But I am a fighter and accepted the offer.

I was discharged on Saturday to the group home and couldn't sleep. I was too excited by this adventure. On Sunday I joined everyone in the dining room for dinner, fearful that I would end up as a welfare bum like many others, having twelve dollars a month spending money, the rest going towards room and board. Right there I decided I would give life a good shot.

Monday morning I returned to the hospital as a day care patient from 9 am to 4 pm. I was seeing my doctor on a regular basis and was revealing things that had lived within me for years. Whatever I did, one priority had to be dealing with reality, life, death, success, failure. These things I had never experienced. I had merely 'survived.' I was experiencing emotions like never before. They were bad, good, hate, love, compassion, need of people, and a general desire to live!

The first problem in therapy is trust in your doctor. People are afraid to reveal intimate secrets to people they don't know, preferring instead to feel ashamed or guilty, afraid that if they confide in him he will not like them and maybe even reject them.

A week after discharge I started the school course. My closest friends from the group home also started on that day. It helped reduce the feeling of insecurity and helped to create a common bond.

It was during this time that I felt a need to really express myself. I thought that maybe if I write down my feelings on paper I wouldn't feel so depressed. I wrote my first poem, called 'Problems.' It was to be my way of coping with reality. I know this sounds strange but I felt inspired to write it. Even today I look at it from time to time to remind myself that there is hope not only for myself but for everyone else.

School was really having an effect on my life. Just getting up early every morning was a pleasure instead of a job. I was receiving a manpower allowance to support myself, and things appeared to be going quite well. But I had a problem with drinking. Let's face it: I was once again avoiding reality. I felt under pressure and this was my way of easing it. Not only did I know that I was jeopardizing my future, but also I couldn't afford it. My girlfriend was lending me money so I could drink. (Two years later I just said to myself that this had to stop, so I stopped it.)

On finishing the course my closest friend and I enrolled in another course designed to give us a career. It was called industrial production orientation and was a real drag.

It was coming into summer when we graduated, so we both enrolled in a trade course called appliance servicing. This was a one-year trade course. I was afraid I wouldn't last through the year. I gave it a good shot though and yes, I graduated. My friend today repairs microwave ovens and is a master at it! I never did find a job in my trade.

Living in the group home was getting a little tough to deal with because as I was getting better the other people in the home seemed to be getting worse. I found this hard to deal with. I decided to stay there until my education was completed.

My doctor and I would sit down for one hour a week discussing and trying to solve my problems. It took one and a half years to control my violent thoughts, yet I would deny that I was angry with anyone. Actually I was very angry at the world for what I felt was a bad deal I got in life. The violent thoughts were my way of dealing with that feeling. Actually when I faced the truth it really hurt. I wasn't really given such a bad deal in life. Life has its ups and its downs. One must learn how to deal with it. I shed a lot of tears while going through this pain. My doctor would not feed into my feeling sorry for myself. It's okay to feel sorry for yourself, but don't prolong it. You've got to go on living your life, and feeling sorry for yourself for a long period could prevent you from doing anything about your life. He was really tough on me. He would not let me get away with denying anything. Honesty with a doctor is the best policy. I found that out.

I wish I could write that I have been successful, but I can't. My thoughts are better and I feel better, but I am poor, haven't got a job yet, and will be going to school again. But I haven't given up!

THIRTEEN

A mother's point of view

The beginning: not understanding

As a parent of a child developing symptoms of schizophrenia,
you cannot understand what is happening. For a long time we
thought our son's strange behavior was due to street drugs,
so we tried to handle it with discipline. We feel now that he
was sick long before the drugs. What we realize now is that
the marijuana temporarily made him feel better, that's why
he used it.

The main question in our minds now is how come we had
so little knowledge? As a mother, I did not need a doctor to
tell me my children had measles or any other fairly common
illness. I had taken first aid courses. I had read about health
care. Why did I never come across articles on schizophrenia
or other mental illnesses that affect young people? With
something that is so serious and touches so many people, why
the secret? I will never understand why mental illnesses are
not as widely publicized as any other illnesses.

The acute attack: Not knowing what to do

Our son had taken a small amount of LSD and was acting what
we thought was very scared. We called our family doctor who

suggested calling a psychiatric hospital. When they heard about the LSD, the hospital told us to go to the addiction centre. We did and followed instructions: twenty-four hours a day of supervised home care, no street drugs, and twice-weekly visits to the doctor. After six weeks of this, our son was getting worse instead of better. The doctor then arranged for entry into the psychiatric hospital.

Finding the right doctor

Finding a good doctor in any field is very difficult. With so many doctors in mental disorders having so many different views about everything, a good psychiatrist is hard to find. Nothing is worse than someone who avoids your questions. Then you always imagine the worst. It was a relief finally to have a doctor who sat down with us and was honest about my son's condition. He answered all our questions and yet left us with lots of hope.

The family's reaction

When a member of the family becomes disturbed like this, a sort of shock sets in at first. You withdraw from friends, not from shame but from a hurt so deep you cannot talk about it. You cannot understand, so how can you hope to have others understand? You don't want to talk about it but you can think of nothing else. Tears run down the face of a husband who never cries, and a wife who cries for any small reason cannot, now when it might help. At this early stage, there is no humor in the world.

When he was hospitalized, it was a very sad time, but at least now we felt he was getting the help he needed so badly. Our own lives were finally able to start again.

How we deal with things in the family now

I try to encourage our son on the good days to get the most out of them. We talk about his day and all the good things he can do and enjoy. On the bad days (we expect there will be many) we want him to understand that they are not a major setback but only a period that will pass. He must get to understand the illness well enough to ignore the bad days and to carry on.

We never lie to our son because we want him to trust us. Our son is not treated as if he is ill. He is an important member of the family with equal rights. We expect him to be well groomed, to be respectful, to be cheerful if possible, and to try to improve. We expect him to let us know when something is wrong and to tell us how he is feeling. We have many, many days when we enjoy his company very much.

You can't tell someone with schizophrenia what to do, you can only encourage. We make no big deal about medicine. If I am not too demanding or too critical, he is usually easy to get along with.

How a relatives' group has helped

I have developed a good understanding of the problems of medication and lack of motivation of the average schizophrenic person. I understand some of the problems of group homes, boarding homes, and the difficult family situations of some patients and families. I know something about services available in the community. I think I have a basic knowledge of some of the symptoms of the illness which are fairly normal and when we should seek help. I realize you cannot push a schizophrenic. You take each day one at a time and you enjoy the good things. You encourage and praise and gently ease things until they are better. The illness seems to go up and down. As parents, we should stay cool and try to keep our family life as normal as possible. You must not allow yourself to become discouraged. I feel families with similar problems can help each other. I would like to help other families as confused as we were to understand how to live a life as normal as possible in spite of the problems of schizophrenia.

Eleven points to remember

1 Never give up, things always improve.
2 Guilt complexes (trying to figure out what you did wrong) are a waste of time. It happened, get on with where you go from here.
3 Do things that make *you* happy.
4 Remember your child is *ill*. He can't help his illness any more than he could if he were paralyzed. Try to keep this in mind. Be patient.
5 Grooming can be a problem, but try to be positive. Tell him how handsome he is when he is well groomed. Leave good clothes handy; hide the old scruffy things he may insist on wearing. Leave shampoo handy and be sure to comment on his clean hair.
6 Encourage his friends to phone or drop in.
7 Never put your son down. He has heard enough of that. Never try to hide him from friends or relatives.
8 Hold on to your religious beliefs; you really need them. (I think this point should be near the top of the list.)
9 Read and seek out all the information you can on your child's illness. Go to mental health lectures put on by mental health associations. Attend lectures at your hospital. Don't hesitate to ask your child's doctor any questions, no matter how ridiculous you think they may sound.
10 Above all, love your child when he is at his worst. Don't wait for him to fulfil your expectations.
11 Take one day at a time. Don't try to solve problems one year or ten years from now.

FOURTEEN

The doctor's dilemma

Schizophrenia is a serious illness and involves a long hard struggle for the patient and those around him. The doctor to whom the care of the patient is assigned has to deal with situations that can at times be very difficult. The real task is to maintain realistic hopefulness in the face of frustrating setbacks and never to 'give up' on a patient. I know that many of my actions are perceived as unwelcome or unpleasant, even though they are intended to help.

My view of schizophrenia obviously determines how I approach care and treatment. I consider schizophrenia a severe disturbance of the brain chemistry, producing very unusual and sometimes frightening experiences. This is the physical, biological basis of the illness. The way one reacts to the psychotic experience is the psychological component. Most people react with fear and mystification at the strangeness of it and at the implication that this is 'crazy.' They are also influenced by the reactions of family, friends, and colleagues.

In my training period I was taught that to be a good psychiatrist one had to be able to understand how the patient felt, for this was the basis of 'therapy'; however, I was told, it is difficult to relate to schizophrenia patients, because they have problems in developing relationships. The implication was:

'Don't bother trying.' I see things differently now. I perceive that the patient has suffered a terrible trauma: the loss of sanity, which we all take so much for granted. No wonder schizophrenics feel sad and hopeless, no wonder they lose their zest for life, no wonder they become afraid to face others, afraid that somehow their madness, their 'difference,' will be seen by others! What a blow to self-esteem and to self-confidence, particularly so when the illness strikes just as people are making plans for the future, for jobs and social and sexual relationships. I can understand that patients will be afraid of me, afraid of being treated primarily as 'mad,' their personhood, their humanity, a distant second. They have every good reason to meet me cautiously.

And what of me? How on earth can I really understand what it is like to be 'mad,' 'crazy,' psychotic? I became aware of my own fear of madness and how it inclines me to keep my distance. This realization has influenced all my subsequent work. There was a subtle change in my thinking from considering my patients as 'schizophrenics' to realizing that they were people, just like me, but afflicted by the illness schizophrenia. I relate to all the people I meet who have schizophrenia as individuals. I want a personal relationship with them and I want them to have a personal relationship with me. Then, together, we can get down to the business of treating the illness.

As a psychiatrist, I know that the best way of dealing with the biological basis of schizophrenia is by the well-adjusted intake of psychotropic medication (neuroleptics). I also know that the medication I prescribe has its side-effects, at times quite troublesome, and I have to be sensitive to the patient's reports of such side-effects. I know that few people relish the idea of having to carry on with treatment procedures ad infinitum. Whether one thinks of schizophrenia, or arthritis, or allergies, or dialysis for kidney failure, the obligation to carry on with a treatment day after day for weeks and months and years is often seen as demoralizing, especially by young people. Not surprisingly, there is a tendency to rebel from time to time against such an indefinite treatment regime. I have to admit that I sympathize with the motives for stopping treatment. At the same time, I owe it to my patients to urge them to continue with long-term treatment.

This creates conflict between my patients and me. I would like to illustrate the dilemma and its resolution by talking about some patients, the first in some detail.

My first contact with Grace dates back seven years; at that time she had already had eight years of intense, severe psychosis, starting at the age of twenty-two. I reviewed her chart and noted that she had spent 38 of the previous 94 months as an inpatient. She had had twelve admissions, some as brief as three days, others as long as 12 months. She had had her longest stay out of hospital (a period of 18 months) while being treated with a long-acting injectable anti-psychotic medication. She was difficult to treat. A pattern developed wherein she would respond very slowly to medication, would get well after a long struggle, have a period of remission, stop her medication, and soon become ill again. Even when taking medication, she was susceptible to depressive episodes.

By the time I started to work with her, she was 29 years old. Her father had died when she was 18, and her mother, who had deserted the family when Grace was only 9, was at that time chronically ill and hospitalized because of multiple sclerosis. Grace was seen by many of the hospital staff as permanently impaired at the time she was referred to me for treatment. She had been told by other doctors to avoid all stress because it might lead to a breakdown. Above all, she had been told not to develop any close relationships with the opposite sex because these were sure to produce a breakdown. It had also been suggested that work was likely to be too much of a stress. For a number of years she had been treated by a psychiatrist who showed a great deal of warmth and interest, but she had developed a child-like, dependent attitude towards him. It became clear to her early on that she was not going to have the same type of relationship with me. Although I had genuine interest and concern for her, I also wanted her to be as independent as possible. Perhaps I risk being disappointed when I set expectations of independence, but I feel it is better to err on the side of too high rather than too low a standard. With Grace I was agreeably surprised because it soon appeared that she was capable of taking on a good deal of responsibility for herself and was becoming fairly self-sufficient. She soon learned a great deal about her illness.

After two years, we got into a series of disagreements. Grace kept requesting reductions in her medication. Since she did not have any side-effects, I tended to resist her requests, but from time to time I found myself going along with her wishes saying, 'Well, we'll take a chance. We'll just have to wait and see how it turns out.' Then I realized that whenever she made these requests she was refusing to accept the reality of her illness. She was hoping that somehow it would just go away and that she would not need the medication. It seemed impossible to convince her, though I continued to try. Another considerable source of worry for me was that at times she thought longingly of being psychotic again. Certain components of a psychosis can appear attractive: the freedom to do the bizarre and the seeming freedom from responsibility. Eventually it came to a confrontation between Grace and me. She wanted me to take her off medication, and I said I could not do this and still fulfil my responsibility as her doctor.

I had moments of self-doubt; perhaps she was right about the medication and about my being too conservative and my anticipating the return of her psychosis where none actually threatened; perhaps, too, it was cruel of me to continue to urge her towards 'health,' when madness might be less of a struggle.

In fact, she stopped her medication on her own and became psychotic a few months later, a pattern that has recurred since. Is insanity a 'reasonable' option that people should be free to choose?

Harry is a thirty-five-year-old man whose schizophrenia had been diagnosed late because his personality difficulties and drug abuse clouded the picture. With him, every drug I pre-scribed he reported as causing serious side-effects without much objective evidence. Clearly, he did not like taking any of the neuroleptic drugs. On one occasion he insisted upon hospi-talization, threatening serious harm to himself and others if I refused to admit him to the ward. It was clear that there was some conflict in his life that he was trying to resolve in this manner, but strenuous attempts on my part to clarify these issues with him were unsuccessful. I was afraid that he would act on his threats if I did not accede to his request for hospi-talization.

He was discharged after only one week, but I worried about the future with this man who does not accept medication but who has proven he can 'blackmail' me into hospitalizing him. On other occasions, Harry has attempted to deal with the conflict between us by asking for a referral to another doctor. He makes initial contact with other physicians, but invariably returns to see me. I often feel that I am fighting a losing battle. To help him remain well, I need to prescribe medication that he is not willing to take. He thus remains unwell, in my care but not under my treatment.

What is the doctor to do under these circumstances? I am never sure how tough to be. One young man, Jim, did poorly during a prolonged hospitalization. We discovered this was because he was smoking marijuana both off and on the ward. Restricting him to the ward and monitoring his visitors led to a marked recovery though it gave the staff the nasty responsibility of being 'jailers.' When he improved, we discussed the dangers of marijuana, and he was again allowed off the ward only to return speedily to marijuana use and a flare-up of his schizophrenia. Frustrated, we decided to restrict him again, but this time he would not accept the restrictions and left the hospital and the city. Naturally, his illness flared within a few days and he was returned to us, still unwilling to give up his marijuana use.

The marijuana abuse presents a threat to other patients who may be given it by Jim; it also makes the staff feel powerless, and when they feel powerless they get angry at me. Should I discharge the patient and face the wrath of the family, or keep him longer, trying to treat him with the aid of an unsympathetic staff? This is one of those tricky situations where I can please the patient by ordering his discharge while angering his family.

Some conflicts turn out well: a patient with whom I had had a warm, collaborative relationship became acutely ill. The family was unable to cope; the patient did not see himself as ill but actually presented a considerable risk to his own safety. I decided to commit the patient involuntarily to the hospital. He insisted that he would never trust me again. Should I go ahead and risk losing the relationship? Or should I go along with the patient and risk a worsening of the illness and possible harm to the patient or to others? I felt almost like a traitor, but I did admit the patient involuntarily. He didn't speak to me at first but, as he improved, he realized what had happened and understood his illness better than before. My action actually cemented our relationship.

Sometimes my own staff may disagree with me about treatment. For example, some of the staff are reluctant to make use of ECT, which I believe to be an effective and humane treatment for certain conditions. It is difficult to proceed with any treatment plan or therapy without staff cohesiveness, so that much time needs to be spent in team conferences and discussions. Patients are quick to sense staff disagreements, and it is often under these circumstances that they refuse treatment.

Patients and their families sometimes seem to get the impression that we doctors have a set treatment approach from which we do not deviate and that we are not sensitive to their concerns and their suggestions. Clearly, for a doctor to behave like that is poor medicine. We cannot always act exactly in accordance with the demands of the patient or family, but we must always be open to their suggestions and willing to incorporate them whenever possible. The central conflict remains: unlike most other illnesses, schizophrenia may affect a person in such a way that he genuinely does not feel in need of treatment.

Schizophrenia presents the physician with many complex problems. It is an area in which relatively few psychiatrists specialize, partly because of these recurrent dilemmas. I have often pondered what makes it worthwhile. I can't be really sure, but I think for me it is a deep concern for those affected by this illness. The illness, schizophrenia, is a common enemy to be conquered. Often it is unconquerable. Frequently, it can only be held at bay, with ultimate victory, it is to be hoped, somewhere in the future. The psychiatrist cannot fight it alone. I have come to realize that I need the help of colleagues skilled in specialized areas, of the individual patients, and of their families. And victory comes closer when I can convey to my patient that the struggle is worth it.

Agencies and services

This is an *alphabetical* listing of agencies and services that may prove useful at different stages of the management of schizophrenia. For families moving to new communities, telephone listings for these services may be obtained in telephone directories. Once you have entered into the network of helpful services, you are more likely to be informed when something new and better becomes available.

Academy of medicine: (might be listed under 'M,' for medical society or 'P' for physicians and surgeons). The academy of medicine will suggest the names of physicians and psychiatric specialists in your neighbourhood. Many psychiatrists subspecialize; for example, they take particular interest in adolescent psychiatry, in family or group or marital therapy, or in schizophrenia. The academy of medicine may be able to provide information about subspecialization.

Alcoholism information and treatment centres: Some sufferers of schizophrenia try for many years to medicate themselves with alcohol in an effort to reduce some of their symptoms. Eventually this may lead to an alcohol problem which may need to be treated in its own right.

Ambulance: Ambulances for transporting ill individuals to hospital are emergency services and are usually listed on the first or second page of the telephone directory.

Associations: Local chapters of medical, psychological, social work, professional psychiatric associations, and self-help associations will be listed under 'Associations.'

Consulates: For travelers abroad, your local consulate will inform you of local facilities.

Crisis or distress centres: These are telephone advice services for crisis situations and are usually listed at the front of telephone books.

Drug addiction information and treatment centres: As with alcohol, drug abuse may become a secondary problem for some people with schizophrenia.

Drug crisis centres: These are detoxification centres for drug and alcohol problems and may be listed under emergency services.

Foundations: There are educational, philanthropic, and research foundations, some of which may be related to work with schizophrenia.

Government services: Everyone should look through the listings under government services for an overview of services provided at the various levels of government. These include income security (family allowances, disability and welfare pensions, unemployment insurance); employment, including handicapped employment; health information and insurance; public health laboratories; mental health centers; psychiatric hospitals; housing; children's services; drug benefits; social services; community centers; legal services (justice of the peace, family law, social work assistance, psychiatric services); coroner's office; police; protection and parole; immigrant reception services; and human rights branch. In the United States the central headquarters for government mental health services are: National Institute of Mental Health, 5600 Fishers Lane, Rockville, Md 20857.

Hospitals: Hospitals may or may not be listed by district. A telephone call to the nearest hospital will provide information about its emergency and psychiatric services. Psychiatric hospitals may be listed separately. A visit to the psychiatric services of different hospitals may help decide which setting is most appropriate for a particular person. Health insurance may cover one type of hospital setting and not another. For information contact: American Hospital Association, 840 North Lake Shore Drive, Chicago, Ill 60611.

Lawyers and legal services: Lawyers are listed by district. Legal aid is available in most communities.

Libraries: Municipal, university, and hospital libraries may be a good source of reading material about schizophrenia.

Mental health associations: City, state or provincial, and national mental health associations are active in different communities. In the United States, contact: Mental Health Association, National Headquarters, 1800 North Kent St, Arlington, Va 22209; in Canada: Canadian Mental Health Association, 2160 Yonge St, Toronto, Ontario M4S 2Z3.

Newspapers: Newspaper articles about new research or new therapeutic programs may direct you to helpful services. Announcements of meetings of local groups, foundations, and associations interested in schizophrenia should be watched for in the local papers. For other publications write to: Public Inquiries Section, National Clearinghouse for Mental Health Information, National Institute of Mental Health, 5600 Fishers Lane, Rockville, Md 20857.

Nurses: Visiting nurse services and public health nurses are available in most communities as well as private nurses.

Nursing home placement services: This is available in some communities.

Personal services: Homemaker, maid, babysitting, and companion services may be required when the family plans a vacation.

Pharmacies: Pharmacists are usually good sources of information about medications and may provide reading material about drugs used in schizophrenia.

Physicians and surgeons: Doctors are listed in telephone directories under this title. There is usually no separate listing for psychiatrists, but the doctor's specialty may be listed after his name. A call to the office will provide information about referral procedure, fees, and the doctor's special interests.

Poison information: In case of overdose, local poison information centers are listed on the first or second page of the telephone directory.

Police: The number for the police is always prominently displayed at the front of the telephone directory.

Radio and television: Science and public service programs are frequently good sources of new information about schizophrenia.

Rehabilitation services: Private services will be listed separately from government-subsidized rehabilitation services.

Religious organizations: Many religious organizations provide hostels, day activity programs, food and clothing supplies to the poor, and counseling services.

Social service organizations: This is an important listing. It includes family and child service agencies; community information services; suicide prevention centers; food, clothing, and shelter for the indigent; housing for special groups, including ex-psychiatric patients; legal services; meals on wheels for shut-ins; translator services for immigrants; special cultural programs for immigrants; self-help groups; and educational services. For information write to: The National Assembly of National Voluntary Health and Social Welfare Organizations, 345 East 46th St, New York, NY 10017.

Family support groups by state

The following family support groups are those known to the National Alliance for the Mentally Ill (National AMI) or the author at the time of publication. Since these groups are proliferating rapidly the list should be considered to be incomplete. For information on recently formed groups contact the National Alliance for the Mentally Ill, 1234 Massachusetts Ave., N.W., Washington, D.C. 20005.

The majority of listed groups are affiliated with National AMI. Those which are listed as chapters of the American Schizophrenia Association or the Huxley Institute are oriented toward an orthomolecular (vitamin and diet) treatment of schizophrenia. A few groups are affiliated with the local chapter of the Mental Health Association (MHA).

ALABAMA

Jefferson-Blount-St. Clair
Mental Health/Mental Retardation
   Authority
3820 Third Ave., S., Suite 100
Birmingham, AL 35222

ALASKA

REACH
% Alaska MHA
808 E St., Suite 216
Anchorage, AK 99501

ARIZONA

Mental Health Advocates
Coalition of Arizona
1245 E. Concorda Dr.
Tempe, AZ 85281

C.O.P.E.
937 Fifth Ave.
Tucson, AZ 85705

ARKANSAS

Arkansas Families for the Mentally Ill
Rte. 1, P.O. Box 49
Edgemont, AR 72204

Help & Hope
4313 W. Markham
Hendrix Hall, Rm 129
Little Rock, AR 72201

Arkansas Parents of Adult Schizophrenics
% Park Hill Presbyterian Church
North Little Rock, AR 72116

CALIFORNIA

Families for Mental Recovery Inc.
Humbolt County
P.O. Box 4404
Arcata, CA 95521

Foothill Family & Friends for Mental
   Recovery
220 Belmont Dr.
Auburn, CA 95663

Barbara Hoover
1817 Ridgewood
Bakersfield, CA 93305

Mental Health Support Group of Kern
County
3017 Pomona
Bakersfield, CA 93305

Association for Mentally Ill of Napa
State Hospital
3438 Lodge Dr.
Belmont, CA 94002

American Schizophrenia Assoc.
Alameda County
2401 Le Conte Ave.
Berkeley, CA 94709

Mental Health Advocates
P.O. Box 324
Cathedral City, CA 92234

Families for Mental Recovery
Yolo County
718 Oeste Dr.
Davis, CA 95616

Advocates For Mentally Ill
Los Angeles County
17140 Burbank Blvd., Unit 107
Encino, CA 91316

Family Alliance for the Mentally
Disabled
P.O. Box 27386
Escondido, CA 92027

Families for Mental Recovery
Alliance for the Mentally Ill
Humboldt County
P.O. Box 6404
Eureka, CA 95501

Families Group of MHA
Fresno County
1759 Fulton St.
Fresno, CA 93721

Families & Friends of the Mentally
Disabled
Riverside County
44981 Viejo Dr.
Hemet, CA 92342

Parents of Mentally Disturbed
San Benito County
#24-1156 San Benito St.
Hollister, CA 95023

Families & Advocates for the Mentally Ill
Napa State Hospital
P.O. Box A
Imola, CA 94558

Darlene Prettyman
Tulare County
18560 Ave 327
Ivanhoe, CA 93235

California AMI
5820 Yorkshire Ave.
La Mesa, CA 92041

Relatives & Friends of the Mentally
Disabled
337 Pine St.
Long Beach, CA 90802

Advocates for the Mentally Ill
3139 Colby Ave.
Los Angeles, CA 90066

Westside and Coastal Friends
Los Angeles County
P.O. Box 241576
Los Angeles, CA 90024

Parent Advocates for Mental Health
61 Morningsun
Mill Valley, CA 94941

Families & Friends of AMI
Stanislaus County
1039 Princeton
Modesto, CA 95350

Families and Friends of Mentally Ill
Stanislaus County
201 Stewart Rd.
Modesto, CA 95350

Parents for Mental and Emotional
Recovery
Contra Costa County
1149 Larch Ave.
Moraga, CA 94556

Parents and Families of Schizophrenics
Napa County
P.O. Box 3494
Napa, CA 94558

South Coast Schizophrenia Association
Orange County
2437 Winward Lane
Newport Beach, CA 92660

CALIFORNIA (*Cont.*)

AMI of Norwalk
11400 Norwalk Blvd.
Norwalk, CA 90650

Families Group of MHA
Alameda County
1801 Adeline St.
Oakland, CA 94607

Families for Mental Recovery
Butte County
P.O. Box 385
Oroville, CA 95926

Families & Friends of the Mentally
    Disabled
Desert Community
39180 Palm Greens Pkwy.
Palm Desert, CA 92260

Relatives & Friends of the Mentally
    Disabled
595 E. Washington Blvd., Apt. K
Pasadena, CA 91104

Foothill Families and Friends for Mental
    Recovery
Auburn County
P.O. Box 234
Penryn, CA 95663

Family Effort, MHA
Sacramento County
2241 Rossmoor Dr.
Rancho Cordova, CA 95670

Friends & Families of the Mentally
    Disabled
Riverside County
5499 Grassy Trail
Riverside, CA 92504

Marin Parent Advocates for Mental
    Health
P.O. Box 1039
Ross, CA 94957

Alliance for the Mentally Ill
3330 Lampsa
San Carlos, CA 94070

Families and Friends of the Mentally Ill
Nancy Olderman
1740 Broadway
San Francisco, CA 94109

San Francisco Schizophrenia Association
San Francisco County
290 7th Ave.
San Francisco, CA 94118

San Francisco Alliance for the
    Mentally Ill
631 Myra Way
San Francisco, CA 94127

Parents of Adult Mentally Ill
Santa Clara County
44 S. Fifth St.
San Jose, CA 95112

San Mateo AMI
P.O. Box 3333
San Mateo, CA 94403

Families & Friends of the Mentally
    Disabled
1515 Capitola Rd.
Santa Cruz, CA 95062

Westside and Coastal Friends
363 20th St.
Santa Monica, CA 90402

Sonoma County AMI
415 Pythian Rd.
Santa Rosa, CA 95405

Family Support Group
San Joaquin County
2853 Calariva Dr.
Stockton, CA 95204

Orange County AMI
17341 Irvine Blvd. No. 105
Tustin, CA 92680

Family & Friends
6740 Kester Ave.
Van Nuys, CA 91405

AMI of Ventura County
P.O. Box AH
Ventura, CA 93002

Mt. Diablo Schizophrenia Association
2857 Ptarmigan Dr., No. 2
Walnut Creek, CA 94595

Parents for Mental & Emotional
    Recovery
P.O. Box 2357
Walnut Creek, CA 94595

Marin Parents for Mental Recovery
Marin County
P.O. Box 419
Woodacre, CA 94973

COLORADO

Aurora Support Group
794 Galena St.
Aurora, CO 80010

Families & Friends of the Mentally Ill
980 6th St.
Boulder, CO 80302

REACH
1232 N. Cooper
Colorado Springs, CO 80905

Significant Others, Adams County
Adams County Mental Health Center
4371 E. 72nd Ave.
Commerce City, CO 80022

Delta Midwestern Mental Health Center
    Group
195 Stafford Ln.
Delta, CO 81416

Family & Friends of the Chronically
    Mentally Ill
4220 Grove St.
Denver, CO 80211

Southwest Denver Family Group
1611 S. Federal Bldg.
Denver, CO 80219

Durango Support Group
P.O. Box 2100
Durango, CO 81301

Friends & Families of the Adult Mentally
    Ill
636 S. College Ave., No. 123
Ft. Collins, CO 80524

Greeley Support Group
3405 23rd St.
Greeley, CO 80631

Colorado Alliance for the Mentally Ill
P.O. Box 28008
Lakewood, CO 80228

Jefferson County Mental Health Center
    Family Group
9808 W. Cedar Ave.
Lakewood, CO 80226

Support, Inc.
11335 W. Exposition Ave.
Lakewood, CO 80226

CONNECTICUT

The Huxley Institute of So. Connecticut
    for Biosocial Research
328 Park Ave.
Bridgeport, CT 06604

Pathways Inc.
40 Doubling Rd.
Greenwich, CT 06830

DISTRICT OF COLUMBIA

Threshold, AMI, DC
P.O. Box 21367
Washington, D.C. 20024

FLORIDA

The Huxley Institute for Biosocial
    Research
1955 N.E. 3rd St.
Deerfield Beach, FL 33441

AMI of North Central Florida
2224 N.W. 15th Ave.
Gainesville, FL 32605

Ms. J. Adams
4500 E. 4th Ave.
Hialeah, CA 33013

Family & Friends Support Group of Palm
    Beach County
666 Laconcia Cir.
Lake Worth, FL 33463

Community AMI
10854 N. Kendall Dr.
Miami, FL 33156

Mental Health Association of Bay
    County
P.O. Box 2245
Panama City, FL 32401

Families Together for Mental Health
1355 Cambridge Dr.
Venice, FL 33595

Family and Friends Support Group
MHA of Palm Beach County
909 Fern St.
West Palm Springs, FL 33401

GEORGIA

Community Friendship, Inc.
85 Renaissance Pkwy, N.E.
Atlanta, GA 30308

AMI Atlantic Chapter
3240 Lucile Ln.
East Point, GA 30344

Central Georgia MH/MR Consortium
P.O. Box 325
Milledgeville, GA 31062

Alliance for the Mentally Ill
30 Chatauchee Crossing
Savannah, GA 31411

Georgia Friends of the Severely Mentally
Ill
1563 Hidden Hills Pkwy.
Stone Mountain, GA 30088

HAWAII

Hawaii Families & Friends of
Schizophrenics Inc.
P.O. Box 25381
Honolulu, HI 96825

Frederick Snyder, M.D.
4778 Kawaihua Rd.
Kapaa, HI 96746

ILLINOIS

Concerned Argonne Scientists
Committee on Mental Dysfunction
Argonne National Lab.
Argonne, IL 60439

North Suburban Chapter
Illinois Schizophrenia Foundation
1510 E. Fremont St.
Arlington Hts., IL 60004

Operation COPE
% Kane-Kendall Mental Health Center
400 Mercy Ln.
Aurora, IL 60506

S.W. Illinois AMI
% Belleville Mental Health Center
200 N. Illinois
Belleville, IL 62220

Recovery, Inc.
Association of Nervous and Former
Mental Patients
116 South Michigan Ave.
Chicago, IL 60603

Vermelien Mental Health & Development
Center
605 N. Logan
Danville, IL 61832

Schizophrenia Association of West
Suburban Chicago
P.O. Box 237
Downers Grove, IL 60515

Tri-County Alliance for the Mentally Ill
111 Sunset Dr.
East Peoria, IL 61611

Illinois Alliance for the Mentally Ill
P.O. Box 1016
Evanston, IL 60204

Manic Depressive Association
P.O. Box 40
Glencoe, IL 60022

Sauk Valley Alliance for the Mentally Ill
1038 N. 8th St.
Rochelle, IL 61068

Alliance for the Mentally Ill of Rock
Island & Mercer County
P.O. Box 933
Rock Island, IL 61201

INDIANA

Fort Wayne Alliance for the Mentally Ill
240 W. Washington Center Rd.
Fort Wayne, IN 46825

Marion County: Together We Learn to
Cope
555 Sunset Blvd.
Greenwood, IN 46142

Mental Health Association in Indiana
Inc.
1433 North Meridian St.
Indianapolis, IN 46202

Parent Information Resource Center
1363 E. 38th St.
Indianapolis, IN 46205

South Bend AMI
1140 E. Ewing
South Bend, IN 46613

IOWA

The Advocates—AMI
3611 Wakonda Dr.
Bettendorf, IA 52722

Dubuque AMI
723 5th Ave., S.E.
Dyersville, IA 52046

Iowa Schizophrenia Association
520 S.E. 1st St., P.O. Box 334
Eagle Grove, IA 50533

North Iowa Transition Center
1907 S. Massachusetts
Mason City, IA 50401

KANSAS

Families for Mental Health
4538 N.E. Meridan Rd.
Topeka, KA 66617

KENTUCKY

Schizophrenia Association of Louisville
7702 Brownwood Dr.
Louisville, KY 40218

Society of Schizophrenia
511 Holmes St.
Terrace Park, KY 45174

LOUISIANA

People's Alliance
1808 Edinburg St.
Baton Rouge, LA 70808

Families and Friends for Mental Health
178 Ronald Blvd.
Lafayette, LA 70503

Family Support Group
500 Walnut St.
New Orleans, LA 70118

Friends of the Psychologically
    Handicapped of Greater New Orleans
6028 Magazine St.
New Orleans, LA 70118

Association for Research in Children's
    Emotional Disorders (ARCED)
P.O. Box 511
Westwego, LA 70094

MAINE

Citizens Interest Group, Inc.
P.O. Box 926
Bangor, ME 04401

Alliance for Troubled Families
Rte. 1, P.O. Box 4420, Pond Rd.
Oakland, ME 04963

Relatives & Friends Together for Support
    (RAFTS)
Star Rte, P.O. Box 390
Poland, ME 04273

AMI of Maine
Box 5196 Station A
Portland, ME 04101

MARYLAND

Mental Health Association of
    Metropolitan Baltimore
323 E. 25th St.
Baltimore, MD 21218

Schizophrenia Association of Greater
    Baltimore
215 N. Tyrone Rd.
Baltimore, MD 21212

Threshold, AMI, Northern Area, Inc.
614 Anneslie Rd.
Baltimore, MD 21212

Threshold, Alliance for the Mentally Ill
7300 Whittier Blvd.
Bethesda, MD 20034

Threshold, Families and Friends of the
    Adult Mentally Ill, Inc.
3701 Saul Rd.
Kensington, MD 20795

Threshold, AMI, Prince Georges County
7509 Newberry Ln.
Lanham, MD 20706

Alliance for the Mentally Ill (AMI)
95 E. Wayne Ave., Apt. 201
Silver Spring, MD 20901

MARYLAND (*Cont.*)
Springfield Hospital Family Support
   Group
% Martin Gross Service Group Bldg.
Springfield Hospital Center
Sykesville, MD 21784

Schizophrenia Association of Greater
   Washington
Wheaton Plaza Office Bldg. N.
Wheaton, MD 20902

MASSACHUSETTS
The Coastal Alliance for the Mentally Ill
P.O. Box 149
Accord, MA 02018

Western Massachusetts AMI Citizens
144 Beckman Dr.
Agawam, MA 01001

Support-Advocacy Group for Families of
   Adult Mentally Ill
15 Maple St.
Ayer, MA 01432

People Support/Advocacy Liberating
   Mental Sickness
14 Colgate Rd.
Beverly, MA 01915

Massachusetts Association of Social
   Clubs (MASC)
Box 9216
Boston, MA 02114

Self-Help Group for Families of the
   Mentally Ill at Massasoit Community
   College
1 Massasoit Blvd.
Brockton, MA 02402

ACCESS
P.O. Box 1865
Fall River, MA 02720

Medfield State Family Alliance
P.O. Box 453
Foxborough, MA 02035

AMI of Middlesex County
P.O. Box 3009
Framingham, MA 01701

Families of Adult Mentally Ill
40 Laurel St.
Leominster, MA 01453

Merrimac Valley Advocacy for Mental
   Health
1018 Osgood St.
North Andover, MA 01845

Citizens Organization Assisting Mental
   Patients, Inc.
4 Ocean St.
North Quincy, MA 02171

Family Support/Advocacy Group of the
   Norfolk Area
151 Cottage St.
Norwood, MA 02062

Amicus of Cape Cod
P.O. Box 962
Osterville, MA 02655

AMI of Eastern Middlesex County
22 Kensington Ave.
Reading, MA 01067

Alliance for the Mentally Ill of
   Cambridge
Middlesex County
P.O. Box 165
Somerville, MA 02144

Alliance for the Mentally Ill of Newton-
   Wellesley
190 Hickory Rd.
Weston, MA 02193

MICHIGAN
Anawim
Robert R. Hartigan, NSJ
Loyola House
2599 Harvard Rd.
Berkley, MI 48072

Cass County Community Mental Health
Family Group
P.O. Box 125
Cassopolis, MI 49031

Citizens for Better Care
1902 Woodward Twr., 10 Witherell
Detroit, MI 48226

Health and Nutrition Awareness
P.O. Box 36331
Detroit, MI 48236

OASIS Fellowship Inc.
P.O. Box 794
East Lansing, MI 48823

Relatives, Inc.
1562 Greencrest
East Lansing, MI 48823

Citizens for Action in Mental Health
(CAMH)
854 Pine Rd., Apt. 254
Essexville, MI 48732

SHARE
P.O. Box 1405
Grand Rapids, MI 49501

SHARE
2371 Valleywood Dr. S.E.
R. 11
Grand Rapids, MI 49506

SHARE
12265 James St.
Holland, MI 49423

OASIS
1212 Parkdale
Lansing, MI 48910

Citizens for Action in Mental Health
(CAMH)
1202 Corrinne St.
Midland, MI 48640

Council of Mental Health Consumers
442 E. Front St.
Traverse City, MI 49684

Relatives of the Mentally Ill
6165 Nicholas Rd.
West Bloomfield, IL 48033

MINNESOTA

REACH
4141 Parklawn #105
Edina, MN 55435

Schizophrenia Association of Minnesota
6950 France Ave., Suite 215
Edina, MN 55435

Mental Health Association of Minnesota
Inc.
6715 Minnetonka Blvd.
Rooms 209-210
St. Louis Park, MN 55426

Mental Health Advocates Coalition of
Minnesota, Inc.
265 Fort Rd.
St. Paul, MN 55102

MISSISSIPPI

Families & Friends of the Mentally Ill
P.O. Box 1286
Hattiesburg, MS 39401

MISSOURI

The National Alliance for the Mentally
Ill (National AMI)
500 E. Polo Dr.
Clayton, MO 63105

Greater Kansas City Chapter AMI
7505 E. 12th St.
Grandview, MO 64111

Alliance for the Mentally Ill
4382 W. Pine Blvd.
St. Louis, MO 63108

Huxley Institute for Biosocial Change
Kimler Building
10424 Lackland Rd.
St. Louis, MO 63114

Schizophrenia Association: St. Louis
Chapter
10426 Lackland Rd.
St. Louis, MO 63114

Schizophrenia Care and Treatment
Society
14 S. Euclid
St. Louis, MO 63108

Alliance for the Mentally Ill
Springfield Missouri Chapter
205 Louis St. Rm 218
Holland Bldg.
Springfield, MO 65806

MONTANA

Great Falls AMI
P.O. Box 3048
Great Falls, MT 59403

North Central Montana Community
Mental Health Center
Holiday Village
Great Falls, MT 59405

Helena AMI
479 S. Parks
Helena, MT 59601

MONTANA (*Cont.*)
A New Beginning for the Mentally
    Disordered
2815 Duncan Dr.
Missoula, MT 59802

NEBRASKA

AMI of Nebraska
Lincoln Center Bldg.
215 Centennial Mall South
Lincoln, NE 68508

NEVADA

Nevada AMI (NAMI)
4220 S. Maryland Pkwy.
Building A, Room 108
Las Vegas, NV 89109

NEW HAMPSHIRE

New Hampshire Division of Mental
    Health
Health and Welfare Building
Hazen Dr.
Concord, NH 03301

Winnipesaukee Advocates for the
    Mentally Ill
35 Ridgewood Ave.
Gilford, NH 03246

Granite State Chapter
American Schizophrenia Association
Box 296
Meredith, NH 03252

AMI of New Hampshire
P.O. Box 544
Peterborough, NH 03458

NEW JERSEY

Focus Mental Health
Delaware House
Wood & Pearl Sts.
Burlington, NJ 08016

FACE
883 Lichtenthal St.
Delran, NJ 08075

Concerned Families for Improved Mental
    Health Services
424 Main St.
East Orange, NJ 07018

Concerned Citizens for Chronic
    Psychiatric Adults
27 Prince St.
Elizabeth, NJ 07208

Concerned Citizens for Chronic
    Psychiatric Adults
P.O. Box 158
Middletown, NJ 07748

FACE
5 New York Ave.
Mt. Holly, NJ 08060

Mental Health Advocacy Group
340 12th St.
Palisades Park, NJ 07650

Family Organization of the Mid-Bergen
    Community Mental Health Center
11 Park Place
Paramus, NJ 07652

TLC
52 Mahoney Rd.
Pennsville, NJ 08070

Schizophrenia Foundation of New Jersey
P.O. Box 25
Skillman, NJ 08558

NEW MEXICO

Community Alliance for Mental Health
12712 Mountain View N.E.
Albuquerque, NM 87123

Community Alliance for Mental Health
P.O. Box 876
Santa Fe, NM 87501

NEW YORK

Relatives
75 New Scotland Ave.
Albany, NY 12208

The Gateposts Foundation Inc.
P.O. Box 526
Bayside, NY 11361

Suffolk County Mental Health
    Association
P.O. Box 519
Brentwood, NY 11717

Friends United to Help the Mentally Ill
50 Nevins St.
Brooklyn, NY 11217

Niagara AMI
610 Sandalwood Drive
Lewiston, NY 14092

Friends & Advocates for Mental Health
9 Maple St.
Liberty, NY 12754

PATH (People Acting Together with
    Hope)
307 Lido Blvd.
Lido Beach, NY 11561

Long Island Schizophrenia Association
1691 Northern Blvd.
Manhasset, NY 11030

Mid-Hudson Chapter, National AMI
Mill House Rd.
Marlboro, NY 12524

Advocates for Mental Health of Northern
    Westchester
Box 155
Mt. Kisco, NY 10549

American Schizophrenia Association
% Huxley Institute
1114 First Ave.
New York, NY 10021

Friends and Advocates of the Mentally Ill
    (FAMI)
NY Self Help Center
240 E. 64th St.
New York, NY 10021

Friends of the New York State
    Psychiatric Institute
722 W. 168th St.
New York, NY 10032

Manhattan State Citizens Group
350 E. 54th St.
New York, NY 10022

New York Friends & Advocates of the
    Mentally Ill
% HAI
1540 Broadway
New York, NY 10036

"Self-Help Reporter," National Self-Help
    Clearing House
Graduate Center/CUNY
33 West 42nd St.
Room 1227
New York, NY 10036

Federation of Parents Organizations
% Rockland Psychiatric Center
Orangeburg, NY 10962

Concerned Citizens of Creedmore
P.O. Box 42
Queens Village, NY 11427

Federation of Parents Organizations for
    the N.Y. State Mentally Disabled
80–45 Winchester Blvd.
Queens Village, NY 11427

Schenectady County Relatives Group
1444 Dean St.
Schenectady, NY 12309

Parents and Relatives of the Mentally Ill
    Supporting Each Other (PROMISE)
423 W. Onondaga St.
Syracuse, NY 13202

Federation of Parents Organizations for
    N.Y. State Mentally Disabled
2175 Wantagh Ave.
Wantagh, NY 11793

Advocacy League for the Mentally Ill of
    Westchester (ALMI)
P.O. Box 1138
White Plains, NY 10602

NORTH CAROLINA

Family to Family
1615 S. College Park
Greensboro, NC 27403

OHIO

Families in Touch
Mental Health Association
1326 Market Ave., North
Canton, OH 44714

North Eastern Ohio Alliance for the
    Mentally Ill
6000 Nob Hill, No. 316
Chagrin Falls, OH 44022

Community Services Planning Project
222 E. Central Pkwy, 502-C
Cincinnati, OH 45202

SOS—CAMI
1207 Elm St.
Cincinnati, OH 45210

OHIO (*Cont.*)
Jewish Family Services
2060 S. Taylor Rd.
Cleveland Hts., OH 44118

Families in Touch
Mental Health Association of Franklin
    County
415 E. Broad St.
Columbus, OH 43215

Families in Touch
Mental Health Association
184 W. Salem Ave.
Dayton, OH 45406

REACH
% Hancock County Mental Health Board
111½ W. Pearl St.
Findlay, OH 45840

Families in Touch
% Mental Health Association
111 Buckeye St.
Hamilton, OH 45011

Kevin Coleman Mental Health Center
275 Martinel Dr.
Kent, OH 44240

Family Resource Centers
799 S. Main St.
Lima, OH 45804

Families in Touch
% The Center
56 Sturges
Mansfield, OH 44902

Families in Touch
Mental Health Association
3 W. Hamtramck St.
Mt. Vernon, OH 43050

Families in Touch
Mental Health Association
65 Messimer Dr.
Newark, OH 43055

Lake Co. Neighboring Project
1657 Mentor Ave.
Painesville, OH 44077

Ohio Association for Emotionally
    Disturbed Children
18013 Fernway Rd.
Shaker Hts., OH 44120

Project TRY
36700 Euclid Ave.
Willoughby, OH 44094

Families in Touch
Mental Health Association
130 W. Second St.
Xenia, OH 45385

Parent Support Group
Mahoning County Transitional Homes
278 Broadway
Youngstown, OH 44504

OKLAHOMA

New Horizons
123 S. 5th
P.O. Box 609
Clinton, OK 73601

American Schizophrenia Association
3808 Grant Ave.
Oklahoma City, OK 73008

REACH
5104 N. Francis, Suite B
Oklahoma City, OK 73118

Families in Touch
5 W. 22nd St.
Tulsa, OK 74114

OREGON

Advocacy and Reassurance for the
    Medically and Emotionally Disabled
    (ARMED)
3308 Southview Dr.
Albany, OR 97321

Family and Friends Support Group
Rte. 1, P.O. Box 1135
Bandon, OR 97411

Taskforce for Mentally and Emotionally
    Disturbed
23975 S.E. Bohna Park
Boring, OR 97009

Coos Bay AMI
4215 Hwy. 101S
Coos Bay, OR 97420

Polk County Mental Health
171 S.E. Uglow, No. 12
Dallas, OR 97338

SAVE A MIND
2981 Willamette
Eugene, OR 97405

Mentally Ill Need Directions (MIND)
Clackamas County Group
6720 Parkway
Gladstone, OR 97027

Josephine County Mental Health Clinic
202 N.W. A St.
Grants Pass, OR 97526

Washington County Mental Health Clinic
2092 East Main
Hillsboro, OR 97112

PREMED
141 S. 17th St., No. 3
Independence, OR 97351

Southern Oregon AMI
P.O. Box 924
Medford, OR 97501

Lincoln County Mental Health Clinic
P.O. Box 1180
Newport, OR 97365

Taskforce for the Mentally &
Emotionally Disabled (TMED)
718 W. Burnside, Rm. 301
Portland, OR 97209

Parents for M.H.
1864 Fir South
Salem, OR 79302

PREMED
3324 Glen Creek Rd. N.W.
Salem, OR 97304

PENNSYLVANIA

Families Unite for Mental Health of
N.W. Pennsylvania
Mercyhurst College Library
Erie, PA 16546

Families United of Orelone PA
% Dr. A. Marsilio
321 Sylvania Ave.
Glenside, PA 19038

Threshold of Lancaster Pa.
% Mental Health Association in
Lancaster County
630 Janet Ave.
Lancaster, PA 17601

National Society for Autistic Children
Greater Pittsburgh Area Chapter
414 Hazel Dr.
Monroville, PA 15146

Families Unite for Mental Health Rights
P.O. Box 126
Oreland, PA 19075

Families & Friends of Norristown State
Hospital
240 Roumfort Rd.
Philadelphia, PA 19119

Combined Parents for Legislative Action
Com. Inc.
Box 15230
Pittsburgh, PA 15230

Families of the Adult Mentally Ill
1623 Denniston Ave.
Pittsburgh, PA 15217

Parents of Adult Mentally Ill
314 Birmingham Ave.
Pittsburgh, PA 15210

Peoples Oakland Mental Health Group
231 Oakland Ave.
Pittsburgh, PA 15213

Main Line Mental Health Group
P.O. Box 243
Radnor, PA 19087

Alliance for the Mentally Ill
Nursing Consultation Center
Rm. 112
Human Development East
Penn State University
University Park, PA 16802

Main Line Mental Health Group
108 E. Lancaster Ave.
Wayne, PA 19087

RHODE ISLAND

Project Reach-Out of Rhode Island
Mental Health Association of Rhode
Island
57 Hope St.
Providence, RI 02906

SOUTH CAROLINA

Families & Friends of the Mentally Ill
P.O. Box 32084
Charleston, SC 29407

Piedmont Family & Friends of the
   Mentally Ill
67 Parkins Lake Rd.
Greenville, SC 29607

SOUTH DAKOTA

Brookings Area REACH
2027 3rd St.
Brookings, SD 57006

Rapid City Area REACH
Mead Pennington County Mental Health
   Association
414 Fairlane B-10
Rapid City, SD 57701

Sioux Falls REACH
South Dakota Mental Health Advocacy
   Project
P.O. Box 618
Sioux Falls, SD 57104

TENNESSEE

Mental Health Association of Tennessee
250 Venture Circle
Nashville, TN 37228

TEXAS

Alliance for Mental Recovery
5731 Charlestown Dr.
Dallas, TX 75230

Alliance for Mental Recovery
4415 Breakwood
Houston, TX 77096

Houston Task Force
2123 Oak Creek
Houston, TX 77017

Reclamation
2502 Waterford
San Antonio, TX 78217

UTAH

Catalyst Families & Friends of the Adult
   Mentally Ill
4183 Parkview Dr.
Salt Lake City, UT 84117

VIRGINIA

Parents Group
1602 Gordon Ave.
Charlottesville, VA 22903

Pathways to Independence
P.O. Box 651
McLean, VA 22101

Richmond Area Schizophrenia
   Foundation
413 Lakewood Dr.
Richmond, VA 23229

Schizophrenia Foundation of Virginia
P.O. Box 2342
Virginia Beach, VA 23452

WASHINGTON

Family Action for the Seriously
   Emotionally Disturbed
505 29th St. S.E.
Auburn, WA 98002

Snohomish County Advocates for the
   Mentally Ill
P.O. Box 2484
4526 Federal Ave.
Everett, WA 98203

Citizens' Guild of Western State Hospital
P.O. Box 94999
Ft. Steilaccom, WA 98494

Cowlitz AMI
P.O. Box 385
Kelso, WA 98626

Peninsula Advocates for the Mentally Ill
87 Garden Club Rd.
Nordland, WA 98358

Family Action for the Seriously
   Emotionally Disturbed
9715 Fruitland Ave., E.
Puyallup, WA 98002

Tri-Cities Advocates for the Mentally Ill
P.O. Box 1135
Richland, WA 99352

Schizophrenia Association of Seattle
506 N. 47th St.
Seattle, WA 98103

Washington Advocates for the Mentally
    Ill
906 E. Shelby
Seattle, WA 98102

Washington State Coalition of Family
    Advocates (State Organization)
% WAMI (Washington Advocates for
    the Mentally Ill)
906 E. Shelby
Seattle, WA 98102

Spokane Alliance for the Mentally Ill
P.O. Box 141141
Spokane, WA 99214

Schizophrenia Support Group
P.O. Box 5353
Vancouver, WA 93663

Yakima Advocates for the Mentally Ill
217 N. 25th Ave.
Yakima, WA 98902

WISCONSIN

AMI Outagamie County
811 E. Pershing St.
Appleton, WI 54912

AMI of Shequamegon Bay
Box 275
Cornucopia, WI 54827

AMI of Sheboygan County
Box 731
Elkhart Lake, WI 53020

AMI, Fond du Lac County
P.O. Box 1007
80 S. Macy
Fond du Lac, WI 54935

AMI of Brown County
1024 Mt. Mary Drive
Green Bay, WI 54301

AMI, Waukesha County
1307 Mariner Drive
Hartland, WI 53029

AMI of Rock County, Inc.
P.O. Box 842
Janesville, WI 53545

AMI, La Crosse County
Rte. 2, Drectrah Rd.
La Crosse, WI 54601

Alliance for the Mentally Ill
Dane County
P.O. Box 1502
Madison, WI 53701

AMI of Manitowoc County
3505 Schroeder Dr.
Manitowoc, WI 54220

Alliance for the Mentally Ill of Greater
    Milwaukee
P.O. Box 16819
Milwaukee, WI 53216

Fox Valley Alliance for the Mentally Ill
1105 Canterbury Dr.
Oshkosh, WI 54901

Fox Valley Alliance for the Mentally Ill
4995 Pickett Rd.
Pickett, WI 54964

AMI of Columbia County
711 W. Cook St.
Portage, WI 53901

AMI of Central Wisconsin
1120 Third St.
Port Edwards, WI 54469

AMI—Racine County
P.O. Box 5202
Racine, WI 53405

AMI of Douglas County
1302 N. 21st St.
Superior, WI 54880

AMI of Wisconsin (State Organization)
Rte. 8, 1997 Highway P.B.
Verona, WI 53593

AMI of Marathon County
201 N. 7th Ave.
Wausau, WI 55401

Suggested reading

Arieti, S. *Understanding and Helping the Schizophrenic* New York: Basic 1979

Bernheim, K. F. and Lewine, R. R. J. *Schizophrenia: Symptoms, Causes, Treatments* New York: Norton 1979

Bernheim, K. F., Lewine, R. R. J., and Beale, C. T. *The Caring Family* New York: Random House 1982

Chamberlin, Judi *On Our Own* New York: McGraw Hill 1978

Gibson, Margaret *The Butterfly Ward* Ottawa: Oberon
— *Considering Her Condition* Toronto: Gage 1978

Green, Hannah *I Never Promised You a Rose Garden* New York: Holt, Rinehart and Winston 1964

Sheehan, S. *Is There No Place on Earth for Me?* New York: Houghton Mifflin 1982

Turner, J., Wing, John, and Creer, Clare *Schizophrenia at Home* London, UK: Institute of Psychiatry 1974

Wing, J. K. ed *Schizophrenia: Toward a New Synthesis* London, UK: Academic Press 1978

Index

alcohol 38
anger 62, 83

causes of schizophrenia 6
child bearing 12–13
clinical record 40
community facilities 32, 79,
  127–31
confidentiality 39, 67, 78
cultural eflects 4, 53
cure for schizophrenia 87

dementia praecox 3
delusions 5
depression 62
diagnosis
– how to make a diagnosis 4
– to tell or not to tell 8–10, 18
diet 36
divorce 68
dopamine 8, 43
double bind 7
drugs 38

employment 81–5
expressed emotion 24, 63, 65

family
– responses 70

– therapy 20–2
finances 22, 68

genetics of schizophrenia 12–13

hallucinations 5
history of schizophrenia 3
hospitalization
– involuntary 73–6
– when and why 14

leaving home 65
legal issues 64, 74

medication 42–50, 57

over-involvement 67

prevalence of schizophrenia 3
psychotherapy 37

relapse in schizophrenia 72
research 88–90
responsibilities of the patient 69

schooling 81–5
self-help groups 38
sex 10–12, 60–2
sheltered employment settings 85

shock treatment 19
signs and symptoms of schizophre-
    nia 4–6, 35, 44
socializing 58
stress and schizophrenia 7, 83
suicide 77
sunscreen lotions 58

tardive dyskinesia 46
therapist choice 32
treatment of schizophrenia
– day care and evening care 25
– diets 36

– family therapy 20–2
– inpatient 14–26
– medication 42–50
– outpatient 27–41
– psychotherapy 37
– shock treatment 19
– vitamins 36

violence 76
visiting in hospital 22, 53
vitamins 36

withdrawal 76